Robert Johnson

Music in American Life

A list of books in the series appears at the end of this book.

Robert Johnson

LOST AND FOUND

Barry Lee Pearson

and

Bill McCulloch

University of Illinois Press
Urbana and Chicago

Library of Congress
Cataloging-in-Publication Data
Pearson, Barry Lee.
Robert Johnson : lost and found /
Barry Lee Pearson and Bill McCulloch.
p.   cm. — (Music in American life)
Includes bibliographical references (p.   )
and index.
ISBN 0-252-02835-X (cloth : alk. paper)
1. Johnson, Robert, d. 1938. 2. Blues musicians—
Mississippi—Biography. I. McCulloch, Bill.
II. Title. III. Series.
ML420.J735P4   2003
782.421643'092—dc21
2002012714

In memory of Kathleen

Contents

Illustrations follow page 52

Preface

In May 2001, just outside Clarksdale, Mississippi, Bill Mc-
Culloch sat in the commissary bar at Hopson Plantation,
chatting with a group that included Tommy Polk, a Nash-
ville songwriter. At some point Bill mentioned this book,
which was then an unfinished manuscript being shopped
to publishers. "So what's it going to be," Tommy wanted to
know, "a definitive biography of Robert Johnson?" No, Bill
said, it would be more along the lines of an investigation—
examining what had been said and written about Johnson
with the aim of showing whether popular legends about
the bluesman, particularly the story that he acquired his
talent in a trade with the devil, were based on reality or
pulled out of thin air. "Awww, no," Polk replied with obvious disappointment, "why would you want to go and do a
thing like that?"

Tommy Polk's spontaneous protest will undoubtedly
turn out to have presaged the reactions of many of Johnson's fans in the Americas, Europe, and Asia. Nobody loves
a debunker, especially when the debunking involves one
of the most captivating legends in American music history. Mindful of that reaction, we start by offering a couple
of disclaimers: First, we did not pursue this investigation
with the idea of razing the Johnson legend and installing
historical truth, whatever that is, in its place. Second, we
had no intention to hand down a stone tablet inscribed
with the one politically correct response to Johnson's art.

The simple reality is that the Johnson legend—the
whole selling-his-soul-at-the-crossroads business—cannot
be eradicated at this late date; it belongs to the people

now, and the fact that people embrace it as a part of American music history is as important as the question of whether it is true. Similarly, blues
fans and researchers alike have found an astonishing variety of ways to
interpret, enjoy, and otherwise respond to Johnson's lyrics and performance styles. Most latter-day fans are unlikely to attach great importance
to the question of whether their responses match the responses of Johnson's original audience or whether their interpretations of Johnson's lyrics are informed by historical context.

That said, we will own up to some biases.

We are suspicious of both the process by which the Johnson legend
appears to have been constructed and the timing of the construction
project. We are incredulous at some of the supposedly informed readings
of Johnson's blues poetry. We cling doggedly to the notion that Johnson
and his music are best understood in the recollections of his peers and
in the context of rural African American culture as it existed during the
lean times of the twenties and thirties.

We hope latter-day fans and interpreters will be at least willing to consider an alternative view of Johnson's life and art. It's always possible that
their enjoyment and appreciation of Johnson will be deepened and enriched, not diminished. In that regard, we urge that this work be considered as a companion and counterpoint to all the other writings about
Johnson. First, it is a chronicle of image making. Second, it is a forum to
address such issues as motivation, methodology, and racial justice. Finally,
it asks a simple question: how did things ever get so out of hand?

Acknowledgments

This book is the product of a collaboration between a folklorist and a journalist. It is also the product of a friendship that began some forty years ago when we discovered a shared interest in the music that had evolved during the first half of the twentieth century in the African American communities of the rural South and Southeast. As the years went by our interest was enriched by encounters and, in a few cases, friendships with artists who were the inheritors of that musical legacy.

While this book focuses mainly on one artist, Robert Johnson, it also attempts to acknowledge the creativity, ingenuity, and fierce independence of all the African American musicians who took their songs and instrumental styles to rural jooks, house parties, suppers, urban clubs, bawdy houses, street corners, and anyplace else they could draw a crowd during the lean days of the Great Depression.

This book draws from interviews with blues musicians conducted over the past thirty-three years in Ann Arbor, Chicago, and throughout the South. The nuts and bolts of this particular project were first assembled during a program at the Smithsonian Festival of American Folklife entitled "Roots of Rhythm and Blues: A Tribute to the Robert Johnson Era" and a similarly titled sound recording published by Columbia (which also happened to be Robert Johnson's label from the sixties on). The goal of that dual presentation—the same as this book's—was to reconnect Robert Johnson and his music to the cultural roots that informed his art. Some of the research and ideas in this book were shared earlier in papers presented to the American Folklore Society in 1992, the Rock and Roll Hall of Fame and Museum in 1998, and the Delta Blues Symposium in 2001.

Judith McCulloh, assistant director and executive editor at the University of Illinois Press, believed in the potential of this book almost from the moment she read our first letter of inquiry. That put her into a very select group. She was a savvy guide throughout the project.

Steve Abbott shared an interview that he and Harry Tufts did with Johnny Shines in 1973. Segrid Pearson O'Dell, Elizabeth Pearson, and Betty Wineke helped prepare material used in the writing of the manuscript. David Dunton, a New York-based literary agent, read an early version of the manuscript, said it ought to be published, and recommended that it be submitted to the University of Illinois Press. M. Carolyn Cooper suggested ways to make the manuscript clearer and more scholarly. Krista Jones, a graphic artist and designer in Columbus, Georgia, consented to the use of her folk-art-style image of Robert Johnson as the basis for a book cover. Jean C. Blackwell, a user-services librarian at the University of North Carolina, conducted searches for references to Robert Johnson in books and periodicals.

Others whose contributions, both direct and indirect, deserve mention include the following: Lawrence Cohen, Frank Driggs, David Edwards, David Evans, Tom Freeland, Alan Greenberg, Edward Komara, Stephen LaVere, Robert "Junior" Lockwood, Jas Obrecht, Diana Parker, Tommy Polk, Ralph Rinzler, Johnny Shines, Chris Strachwitz, Henry Townsend, Paul Vernon, Gayle Dean Wardlow, and Jon Waxman, all of whom gave willingly of their time, counsel, and knowledge as this project moved through the various transitions leading to publication.

And finally, thanks to John Cephas, Craig Jones, William Lightfoot, Charlie Musselwhite, Rob Riley, Peter Seiler, Robert Terwilliger, and Phil Wiggins, legendary musicians one and all.

Robert Johnson

1 The Making of a Paper Trail

> The literature on Johnson, already voluminous and still piling up, reads like an ongoing detective novel with Johnson . . . as the missing person whose trail leads everywhere but to himself."
>
> —Francis Davis, *The History of the Blues*

Lord knows, he tried to be a family man, but something always drew him back—or drove him back—to the road. He spent most of his adult life traveling from town to town, playing guitar and singing for gatherings on street corners, at suppers and house parties, and in rural roadhouses and urban clubs. Although his travels took him to most regions of the United States, he remained a virtual unknown outside the racially segregated venues of the Deep South, where his music was most at home. He made a few records, but only one of them sold very well—mainly in the South. He died in 1938, three months after his twenty-seventh birthday.

Decades after his death this slightly built African American drifter named Robert Johnson rose from obscurity to become an all-American musical icon, the best-known although least understood exemplar of the Mississippi Delta blues tradition. He was celebrated by a small circle of jazz buffs who discovered his recordings in the thirties and forties and thought his music echoed the pure origins of jazz. He was a revered cult figure to a new generation of folk-music fans who discovered blues in the sixties. Later he was among the first thirteen musicians to be inducted into the Rock and Roll Hall of Fame. He won a Grammy Award. He was lionized in novels, screenplays, books, and hundreds of articles. Because of his exalted status, his life and music were researched, reviewed, and analyzed with singular intensity. Starting with the fledgling efforts of Samuel Charters in the fifties, a determined procession of researchers—Pete Welding, Gayle Dean Wardlow, Stephen Calt, Mack McCormick, Peter Guralnick, Stephen LaVere, and others—tracked down bits and pieces of information about Johnson. People who had actually known Johnson, particularly the blues musicians who had heard him and worked with him, were exhaustively debriefed in scores of interviews. As a result, we now have access to more facts, documents, and first-person recollections about Robert Johnson than we have about all but a handful of other blues musicians.

Yet we are confronted with a paradox. Even those most familiar with the facts—indeed, some of the researchers who helped dig out the facts—have too often misrepresented Johnson as a mythic figure, an enigma. In some respects the biographical images that have emerged since Johnson's death have moved progressively farther into romantic fantasy even as the published body of factual information has grown.

In the earliest attempts to construct a picture of Johnson, he was portrayed as an authentic folk genius, a shy farmhand who had never known life away from the plantation and whose enormous talent found its way to a recording studio largely by a stroke of luck. In later biographical sketches Johnson was transformed into something akin to a demented street person, a deeply troubled loner driven by forces dark enough to make him potentially violent who wandered from place to place revealing through his music the psychic pain and inner demons that tormented him.

Discussions of Johnson's music paralleled these early biographical images. They presented his art as the last and most highly evolved example of an older style—a dying echo of one of the primitive building blocks from which jazz was constructed; as a breathtaking and sometimes eerie departure from the older style; and finally, as the first faint rumblings of the rock-and-roll revolution.

The image of Johnson prevailing today—the Johnson legend—borders on allegory. He has been cast as the unsophisticated but ambitious young musician who, in one fateful moment, sells his soul to the devil, or at least chooses to believe he has, and who thereafter flashes all too briefly across the American musical landscape, a genius possessed by self-destructive impulses who leaves behind a small but utterly singular musical legacy: blues lyrics laced with Faustian imagery, recordings of a voice imbued with supernatural foreboding, and little else. This is truly the stuff of legend. But it is not Robert Johnson. It is doubtful that any of Johnson's wives, friends, or fellow musicians would recognize him based on such a composite. So where did all the romantic fantasy come from?

To find out, we must examine a paper trail that spans over sixty years. The trail, sad to say, is strewn with examples of dubious research, far-fetched interpretation, and unsupported assertion. But it is informative to study how misinformation about Johnson was recycled, how myth became accepted as fact, and most significantly, how Johnson's most respected chroniclers too often shaped or invented facts to serve their own needs.

For the most part we will examine the paper trail chronologically, showing how each of the biographical images of Robert Johnson emerged and how the various images evolved, faded, or intermingled with the passing of time. To provide a reality check, we will occasionally visit the recollections of musicians and others who knew Johnson to see whether their memories support or contradict the published biographical images. In the end, we believe, the evidence will show that the best-known images of Johnson were the product of ignorance and economics: white ignorance about African American traditions and culture and the desire to find ways to market Johnson's music to new generations of mostly white blues fans long after Johnson's death.

As we review the biographical reconstructions of Robert Johnson, four patterns emerge:

First, a small core of anecdotes became the primary grist for Johnson's early biographers. The anecdotes survived for decades, even though they tended to portray Johnson in ways that were clearly at odds with who he really was.

Second, because they found it difficult to unearth factual information about Johnson, early biographers chose to characterize the artist as a riddle or mystery, at times a vaguely menacing mystery. The artist-as-enigma approach became so much a part of the Johnson legend that it survives to this day, even in the face of evidence to the contrary.

Third, caught in a factual vacuum, each new wave of biographers rewrote what had been written by earlier writers. The only way to freshen the same old stories about Johnson (and avoid obvious plagiarism) was to resort to escalating levels of excited prose. Misinformation and dubious anecdotes were thus compounded by hyperbole. (A few of Johnson's fellow musicians also were prone to embroidery and invention.)

And fourth, having recycled and exhausted the limited biographical material, some researchers turned to Johnson's song lyrics as the key to his life and personality. Most of these writers knew very little about Johnson's culture or the blues tradition, so they applied their own cultural references to the lyrics, often with reckless abandon. In the process they removed Johnson from any relevant context and churned out reams of subjective "imaginings" about what his life might have been and what his songs might mean. These flawed analyses now constitute a disproportionate share of the literature on Johnson.

The crowning result of all this was reverse alchemy. Valuable information about Johnson and his music was debased, distorted, or just ignored; a counterfeit story line emerged in which Johnson was cast as a twentieth-century Faust, relinquishing his soul and perhaps his sanity in an unholy trade for musical knowledge.

Why was Johnson—and *only* Johnson—treated this way? Even after examining the paper trail and weighing all the evidence, it is doubtful that we can fully answer that question. Nor can we fully explain why his presence and music affect us so deeply, for he truly does rank among the finest blues poets ever. But we can begin to show how the Johnson legend was created, who created it, and why it has always been so difficult for us to accept Robert Johnson's simple humanity and artistic quality at face value.

2   Our Hero

I got rambling . . . I got rambling all on my mind.
  —Robert Johnson, "Rambling on My Mind" (1936)

Even as the body of romantic mythology about Robert Johnson grew in the decades following his death, so, too, did the volume of carefully researched facts and first-person recollections. For readers who know little or nothing about this storied blues artist, this chapter offers a short biographical outline. Based on public records, court documents, the memories of Johnson's contemporaries, and the work of such biographers as Stephen Calt and Gayle Dean Wardlow, Mack McCormick, Peter Guralnick, Jas Obrecht, Stephen LaVere, and Tom Freeland, the outline is intended to provide helpful reference points for the investigation that follows. Readers who are familiar with the generally accepted facts and suppositions about Johnson's life may choose to skip to chapter 3.

One cautionary note: In the early years of blues scholarship, the literature was often replete with dubious information either recycled from dubious prior research or conjectured from sparse facts. We made a diligent effort throughout this book to avoid presenting such information as fact, but we are not naïve enough to believe that we weren't fooled in a number of instances.

Most accounts say that Robert Leroy Johnson was born in Hazlehurst, Mississippi, on May 8, 1911,[1] the illegitimate son of Julia Major Dodds and Noah Johnson, a farmhand. By the time Robert was born, Julia Dodds already had ten children by her husband, Charles Dodds, but most of them were no longer living in Hazlehurst. They had moved to Memphis to be with Charles Dodds, who had fled from Hazlehurst in 1909 or 1910 after getting into a bitter dispute with another local landowner and losing his farm in a mortgage foreclosure. After moving Dodds changed his last name to Spencer and started a new family made up of all the children from his marriage to Julia plus two children he had fathered with a woman who had been his mistress back in Hazlehurst.

Robert went to Memphis to live with Spencer around the age of three. He returned to Mississippi about four years later to live with his mother and her second husband near Robinsonville, in the far northwest corner of the state. He attended the Indian Creek School but was hampered by poor eyesight, possibly caused by a "defective" left eye that fellow musicians described many years later. One of Johnson's friends from that era recalled that young Robert was often gone for long periods, probably because he was still living part time with Spencer in Memphis.

Some accounts say Robert's first stringed instrument was a diddley bow, traditionally made by stretching a strand or two of wire between nails hammered into the side of a shed or some other wood structure. The youngster later picked up a few guitar chords from one of his brothers while in Memphis, and his interest in music grew as he was exposed to the playing of such early blues guitarists as Charley Patton, Ernest "Whiskey Red" Brown, Harvey "Hard Rock" Glenn, and Myles Robson.[2] His desire to earn a living as a musician was fueled by exposure to the rigors of farmwork—something he grudgingly tried when he lived with his mother and step-father and again later after his marriage to Virginia Travis in 1929, just as the Great Depression, already a fact of life in rural America, began to cripple most sectors of the U.S. economy.

In April 1930 Johnson's wife, who was still in her teens, experienced complications during the birth of her first child. Both she and the baby died.

It was also around 1930 that one of the most powerful early blues artists, Son House, came to Robinsonville and began playing what he described as "Saturday night balls" in partnership with Willie Brown, also a fine blues singer and guitarist. House later remembered Johnson as a "little boy" who could play a passable harmonica but who would "drive the people nuts" whenever he tried to play guitar at parties, something he often did when House and Brown took breaks.

In late 1930 or early 1931 Johnson moved to the area around Martinsville, a lumber town in the southern part of Mississippi, not far from his birthplace, supposedly looking for his real father.[3] Using the music he had absorbed from House and Brown, he began playing house parties and jook joints[4]—rural markets or general stores that doubled as nightclubs on weekends—with a new guitar mentor, Ike Zinnerman. (A recently discovered source, interviewed by Gayle Wardlow, recalled that Ike had a brother, Herman, who could also play guitar, and the two often played together, so Johnson may have learned from both of them.)[5] Johnson began seeing a young woman, Vergie Mae Smith, who gave birth to a son in December 1931; decades later Smith's child was ruled to be Johnson's only legal heir. While living in the Martinsville area, Johnson also began a relationship with Calletta Craft, an older woman who had been married twice before and who had three children. Johnson and Craft were married in May 1931, not long after Vergie Smith became pregnant. In 1932 the couple moved north to the Delta town of Clarksdale, where Calletta fell on poor health and soon was abandoned by Johnson.

Most accounts agree that at this point Johnson took to the road, launching the itinerant existence that would be his trademark for the next few years. But some accounts also suggest that Johnson paused at least long enough to return to Robinsonville, where he again encountered House and Brown at a weekend party. As House recalled it many years later, he and Brown were impressed by the progress Johnson had made as a guitar player and singer—a quantum leap that would eventually stoke the imaginations of researchers and critics alike as they studied Johnson's life and art.

Vergie Smith claimed many years afterward that Johnson returned to the Martinsville area twice in 1932, hoping to persuade her to travel with him. She said she refused and never saw Johnson again.

Now well on his way to becoming a polished professional, Johnson established a base in Helena, Arkansas, and worked extensively throughout the South as a walking musician,[6] traveling sometimes alone and sometimes with other guitar players, such as Johnny Shines or Calvin Frazier. He frequently traveled and played under assumed names, a habit that complicated later efforts to construct an accurate biography.

It was during this time, between his late teens and midtwenties, that Johnson began to absorb, blend, and refine particular stylistic nuances—drawn from piano as well as guitar—that would eventually help redefine blues for a new generation of musicians who left the South and moved to St. Louis, Detroit, and most prominently, Chicago.

It was also during this time that Johnson entered a common-law relationship with Estella Coleman in Helena. Her son, Robert Lockwood, learned guitar from Johnson and eventually became a prominent bluesman in his own right; performing as Robert "Junior" Lockwood, he continued to play much of Johnson's repertoire along with his own for decades after Johnson's death.

Although Johnson was well known in Arkansas, Mississippi, and Tennessee by the midthirties, he yearned to record, as many of his mentors and influences already had. So, according to most accounts, he traveled to Jackson, Mississippi, to audition for H. C. Speir, a music-store owner whose ear for talent had led to recording sessions for a veritable who's who of important regional blues artists during the twenties and thirties.[7] Speir put Johnson in touch with Ernie Oertle, a salesman and scout for the American Record Corporation (ARC), and Oertle twice took (or sent) Johnson to Texas to record.

In Texas Johnson was turned over to Don Law, British-born regional manager for ARC. Law, ten years Johnson's senior, had immigrated to the United States in 1924, securing work in Dallas with Brunswick Records, which later became part of ARC and, still later, of Columbia. Johnson's recordings were issued first on ARC, then on Vocalion (a label owned by ARC), and finally, long after Johnson's death, on Columbia.

Under Law's supervision Johnson began recording on November 23, 1936, in a San Antonio hotel.[8] All told he recorded sixteen songs in three sessions spread over five days. Included among the songs was "Terraplane Blues," the closest he ever came to a genuine hit during his lifetime. Seven months later in Dallas, with Law again serving as A&R supervisor,[9] Johnson recorded thirteen songs, ten of them in a single session in sweltering heat on June 20. Nearly a dozen songs from the Dallas sessions were issued, though none of them ever matched the popularity of "Terraplane."

After the two June sessions in 1937, Johnson resumed the life of an itinerant musician, turning up later that year in Greenwood, Mississippi, which may have been a regular summer stop for him. Blues artist David "Honeyboy" Edwards, then about twenty-two, was living in Greenwood and recalled that Johnson created quite a stir while playing on the street one afternoon when he was asked if he knew "Terraplane Blues." Johnson's rendition made it clear to everyone within earshot that he was indeed the musician who had made the popular record. Johnson was showered with small change.[10]

According to Edwards, Johnson returned to Greenwood the following summer and was offered a gig playing on two consecutive Saturday nights at a country jook located in a convenience store (or "grab-all," as some locals called it) known as the Three Forks, outside Greenwood.[11] Most narratives used to say that Johnson was hired to play the first two Saturdays in August, but Johnson's death certificate states that he last worked as a musician in July, which is plausible given all the evidence now in hand.

After the first Saturday, Edwards said, Johnson began seeing the wife of the man who owned the jook.[12] It was a typically brazen act on Johnson's part, but in this instance, a fatal one. While the facts about Johnson's death and burial remain shrouded by legend and invention, the testimony of Edwards and other musicians suggests that Johnson was slipped some poisoned whiskey at the jook on the second Saturday night, and he became too sick to play.[13] Around two in the morning he was moved to a bed or pallet in the jook. From this point on, the accounts differ.

One witness who claimed to have been at the jook said that Johnson was laid out on "a little old piece of cotton cloth," died at the jook early Sunday morning, and was buried by the county on Monday.[14] According to other reports, a man known as Tush Hog drove Johnson from the jook back to the "Baptist Town" section of Greenwood, where he watched over Johnson for the next two days before the musician died on Tuesday.[15]

Newer research by Stephen LaVere and others suggests that Johnson had been staying at a rooming house in Baptist Town that July and that he was taken there after he became sick. Johnson actually survived the poisoning, according to LaVere's findings, but was so debilitated that he contracted an infection, most likely pneumonia, for which there was no cure at that time. As the infection progressed, Johnson was moved from the rooming house to Tush Hog's residence, which was located not in Baptist Town but on Star of the West Plantation, just north of town. There, on August 16, 1938, Johnson died. His body probably was buried at Little Zion M. B. Church, a little under two miles from the residence where he died. A monument, commissioned by LaVere, now stands in the church-yard.[16]

There is conflicting testimony as to whether any members of Johnson's family were able to get to Greenwood for the burial, but most sources agree that his sister Carrie eventually claimed his guitar and other belongings. Among the items supposedly found at Tush Hog's residence was a note, which some researchers believe was handwritten by Johnson. It read, "Jesus of Nazareth, King of Jerusalem, I know that my Redeemer liveth and that He will call me from the Grave."

Although most researchers and many of Johnson's contemporaries eventually concluded that Johnson had been the victim of foul play, no one was ever charged in connection with the death.

By the time Johnson died, his recordings had attracted the attention of a small group of New York–based music critics and jazz promoters. Their well-intentioned efforts to construct a biography of the blues artist focused on information gleaned from his two recording sessions, stories about his death, and clues combed from his song lyrics. From a historian's point of view, the results were calamitous.

3   The Anecdotes

I knew him only from his blues records and from the tall,
exciting tales the recording engineers and supervisors used
to bring about him from ... Dallas and San Antonio.

—John Hammond

Don Law, the British producer who recorded Johnson, was
a key source of early information about the blues artist.
H. C. Speir and Ernie Oertle, the two talent scouts who put
Johnson in touch with Law, also provided recollections,
but Law was the initial and primary source. His anecdotes,
unchallenged for thirty years, were recycled over and over
again by Johnson's early biographers.

By the time he recorded Johnson, Law had already presided over a number of blues sessions in both Mississippi
and Texas. He had also tried his hand at promoting blues
to merchants who sold "race records," the common term at
that time for music aimed at the African American market.
Law is best known, however, for his recording of country
and western music, so most of the testimony concerning
his approach to A&R work comes from country music artists. Ray Price, for one, said Law was a producer who would
"let an artist be an artist." In that vein, Law was remembered
for letting members of the Bob Wills band record in their
underwear on a particularly hot day, for letting that same
band play louder than usual at their request, and for let-

ting certain artists loose the muse with whiskey—all in the name of getting as much material as possible out of each session.[1]

We do not know whether Johnson's sessions were similarly equitable, whether Johnson, too, recorded in his underwear or under the influence of alcohol. But legend leads us to believe that Johnson set Law's recording microphone in a corner of the room and played facing the wall. Even if Law misinterpreted this move, as evidence suggests he did, the fact that he allowed it lends credence to his reputation for cooperation and collaboration. Other evidence, though, suggests that Law considered Johnson to be naïve and unprofessional and was, to some degree, exasperated by Johnson's out-of-studio behavior.

Given all the evidence, it seems fair to say that Law was not a reliable source of information about Robert Johnson. The blues researcher and record producer Samuel Charters, for example, relied heavily on Law's recollections of the 1936 sessions, citing Law's testimony that Johnson "was very reticent and very shy. This was the first time he'd been to what he considered a big city, the first time he had ever been off the plantation."[2] Law apparently conveyed a similar impression to impresario John H. Hammond Jr., who wanted Johnson to perform in concert at Carnegie Hall in New York. Law argued that Johnson was too shy and would die of fright.[3]

In fact, Johnson was an accomplished street performer, earning a living in the middle of the depression by engaging and entertaining strangers. He was also remembered for his ability to connect with jook-joint audiences. And he was already well traveled. As a walking musician, he followed an orbit that included the Delta and the connecting cities of Jackson, Mississippi; Helena and West Memphis, Arkansas; Memphis; and St. Louis. Occasionally trips took him as far as Canada and Brooklyn, New York. His on-again, off-again partner Johnny Shines recalled the wanderings:

> Robert liked to travel. You could wake up anytime of night and say "Let's go" and he was ready. He never asked you where or why or anything. He would get up and get dressed and get ready to go. And I often say, I guess him and I were the first hippies because we didn't care when, where or how. If we wanted to go someplace, we went. We

didn't care how we went. We'd ride, walk. If you asked us where we were going we didn't know. Just anywhere.
"Are you going north?"
"Yeah."
"Get in."
We'd get in and go.[4]

As for Johnson's shyness, Law appears to have based this impression at least in part on Johnson's preference for facing the wall while recording. Law turned this into a touching anecdote, which eventually grew into a blues legend, in which he portrayed Johnson as so shy he could play only by turning his back on a group of Mexican musicians who were scheduled to record at the same session. But Johnny Shines, among other contemporaries, said this was typical of Johnson's demeanor around musicians: "So Robert was playing some of the stuff that I wanted to play, and making chords that I was lacking. . . . So I began to follow him around, you know, to hear him play—not to hear him play but to watch him play. And he would catch me watching him, looking at him, watching his fingers, and he turned his back on me. And that went on for close to a year. He'd catch me watching him and he'd walk away. He'd just disappear. Just got swallowed up in the crowd."[5] So what Law interpreted as stage fright was more likely possessiveness: Johnson wanted to prevent other guitar players from stealing his licks. (Several musicians have suggested an alternative explanation, that Johnson preferred the acoustics he got when playing toward the wall.)

Interestingly, Law's impression of Johnson as a raw primitive who would be out of place in a big city remained unshaken even in the face of two incidents that later became part of Law's anecdotal legacy. The British A&R man claimed his dinner was interrupted by two calls from Johnson the night before the initial recording session. First Johnson got into a scrape with local police, was beaten and jailed, and called to ask for bail money. Later he needed money to pay a prostitute.[6]

Even if taken with the requisite grain of salt, such anecdotes seem to describe someone who was street hardened and more than a little worldly. That's exactly how Johnson was described many years later by Law's son, Don Law Jr., who said it was obvious, at least in retrospect, that

Johnson was a pretty slick operator who "knew how to move around."[7] But in 1936 the apparent inconsistency did not prompt the senior Law to revise his impressions of Johnson to any noticeable degree, nor did it daunt the researchers who later relied on Law's testimony.

Law's impressions of the unsullied rustic were passed along to John Hammond and resurfaced in a public elegy in Hammond's 1938 Carnegie Hall production "From Spirituals to Swing." Hammond wanted Johnson for the New York show but learned from the ARC salesman and talent scout Oertle that he had recently died. In his onstage elegy Hammond told the audience: "Robert Johnson was going to be the big surprise of the evening. I knew him only from his blues records and from the tall, exciting tales the recording engineers and supervisors used to bring about him from the improvised studios in Dallas and San Antonio. I don't believe that Johnson had ever worked as a professional musician anywhere, and it still knocks me over when I think of how lucky it is that a talent like his ever found his way to phonograph records."[8]

A fetching story, but as we now know, Johnson was a professional of several years' standing who found his way to phonograph records less by luck than by using the right connections. Anyway, Hammond went on: "Johnson died last week at the precise moment when Vocalion scouts finally reached him and told him that he was booked to appear at Carnegie Hall on December 23."

Dramatic, but not true. No evidence suggests that Vocalion scouts approached Johnson on his deathbed. Rather, Oertle heard through the grapevine that Johnson was dead and passed the word to Hammond, who, in the spirit of the "tall, exciting tales" he so enjoyed, couldn't resist touching up the artist's demise with a little imagined drama.[9]

Hammond was not alone in this regard.

Because Robert Johnson was not well known outside the African American community, news of his death traveled mainly by word of mouth. Son House, one of Johnson's early mentors, said he heard first that Johnson had been stabbed to death and then that he had been poisoned. Johnny Shines, Johnson's occasional traveling companion, said he first heard that Johnson had died in Eudora, Mississippi, that "black arts" were somehow involved, and that Johnson had died on his hands and knees, barking like a dog.[10] Few people seemed to know exactly when and where the death had occurred. As late as 1959, when John Hammond's "Spirituals to Swing" concerts were reissued on vinyl,[11] Hammond's liner notes reported that Johnson had been "murdered in a Mississippi barroom brawl" shortly after he signed to appear at the 1938 concert (but omitted the deathbed scene). That same year Samuel Charters wrote that Johnson had been murdered in San Antonio in 1937. Wrong place, wrong year. But Charters, unlike some others, should not be found guilty of fanciful invention—at least not on this particular score. Charters believed that San Antonio was the last place Johnson had been seen by recording personnel, who were then still considered a reliable source of information, and he had heard from the musicians' grapevine that Johnson had been murdered. His detective work was faulty, but he was making a legitimate attempt to piece together the sparse bits of real information that were available in the late fifties.[12] In the early sixties the researcher and record executive Nick Perls told another researcher that he had interviewed a "Negro named Sol Henderson in Robbinsonville [*sic*] Mississippi" who claimed he and Johnson played together in Friars Point in 1937 or 1938 when Johnson was killed, stabbed by a girlfriend he had slapped, and that he died on a Sunday.[13] The English-language version of the German critic Joachim Berendt's work *The Jazz Book: From New Orleans to Rock and Free Jazz,* published in 1975, identified Johnson as a bluesman who came from Mississippi and was poisoned in Texas.[14] And Hammond's autobiography, published in 1977, reported that Johnson "had been killed by his girl friend."[15]

David "Honeyboy" Edwards claimed to have been present when Robert Johnson was poisoned. Although he may or may not have been present when Johnson died, he was probably one of the early disseminators of the news. He said Johnson drank whiskey that had been poisoned and became so ill that he was unable to continue entertaining a full house at the Three Forks jook where he had been hired to play: "Now the people was drunk and began to think he was bullshitting them. 'Aw, come on, come on.' But the man was sick. He was poisoned to death, but the other people out there, they didn't know it. Man's laying over the guitar, he's trying to play it, but he solid just can't. And the people, like everybody, got silent, dead. Walkin around cause the man was sick. And Robert died about one-thirty or two. . . . And the state, the county, buried Robert. The county buried him on Monday."[16] Note that Edwards did not recall seeing any scouts from Vocalion.

This account, taken from a 1978 interview, was similar to one Edwards gave to the jazz critic Pete Welding in the sixties. In these early accounts Edwards evidently missed or forgot some details concerning where and how long the poisoned Johnson suffered before dying. But in later tellings of the story Edwards became more specific, though not always more accurate, about the time and place of death, recalling, for example, that he went to visit Johnson at a house near Greenwood the day before the artist died and found him "crawling around . . . slobbering and going on and heaving up." In one of the later versions Edwards even pointed to a possible cause of death, opining that Johnson might have been slipped a dose of "passagreen," supposedly a toxic liquid extracted from mothballs and often used, depending on the authority, as a douche. (As we will show later, Edwards became more expansive and more specific about other key aspects of the Johnson legend as well, not just the artist's death).

No summary of Johnson death notices would be complete without mention of the harmonica virtuoso Sonny Boy Williamson no. 2, also known as Aleck Miller, Rice Miller, Willie Miller, Biscuit Miller, Footsie, and several other names. Ever the con man, Williamson told fellow musicians that he, too, had been there at the jook joint, admonishing Johnson never to drink from any whiskey bottle he had not opened himself and even knocking a suspicious bottle right out of Johnson's hands before he could drink from it. After Johnson finally drank from a bottle of doctored moonshine, Williamson said, he comforted Johnson in his arms as the poisoned artist breathed his last breath.

Depending on the audience, Williamson could offer two separate and distinct accounts of Johnson's death and was capable of embellishing either account. The most familiar account was the one just noted, which had Johnson dying while cradled in Williamson's arms. In the other Johnson died in an ambulance headed from Memphis, Tennessee, to Jackson, Mississippi, and he died because "he drank too much."[17]

In fact, there's testimony that Williamson was at the jook that Saturday night, hired as part of the evening's entertainment. But there is no evidence that he stayed with Johnson until the end. Nor is there any evidence that Johnson was ever transported by ambulance. Like so many others, Sonny Boy just couldn't resist adding a personal dramatic touch to his own footnote in the Johnson legend.

It wasn't until 1973, thirty-five years after the fact, that Johnson's death certificate was located in the records of the Mississippi state registrar of vital statistics. It confirmed that Robert L. Johnson, a musician, had died "outside" Greenwood on August 16, 1938—a Tuesday—but listed no cause of death. Years later extensive notations were discovered on the *back* of the certificate. From these it was learned that the white owner of the property where Johnson had died believed the cause of death to be syphilis; that a doctor at the state charity hospital had theorized later that congenital syphilis, coupled with heavy drinking, could have triggered a fatal aneurysm; and, as a third possibility, that a combination of poison and moonshine could have led to pneumonia.[18]

Questions about the sequence of events before and after Johnson's death remained unanswered for more than sixty years. As we have seen, however, the missing facts often seemed to be an inducement to speculation and invention. That pattern would soon become a prominent feature in the writing on Johnson. Something similar happened with Don Law's colorful anecdotes and inaccurate impressions. They lived on for decades, eventually becoming part of the liner-note mythology that helped introduce and explain Johnson to impressionable middle-class fans who discovered him in the sixties and later.

4 Early Notices

Watch your close friend, baby, then your enemies can't do
you no wrong.
   —Robert Johnson, "When You Got a Good Friend" (1936)

The first extended print reference to Robert Johnson outside of music industry communications appeared in the
March 2, 1937, issue of *The New Masses,* a left-wing peri-
odical based in New York.[1] Following notices for two plays,
titled *Chains* and *Marching Song,* a lecture on "The Moscow
Treason Trial," a fund-raiser to aid leftist opposition in Spain,
and ads for tours of the Soviet Union, a column by Henry
Johnson—possibly a pen name for the jazz record producer and critic John H. Hammond Jr.—heralded the arrival
of a new blues voice: "We cannot help but call your attention to the greatest Negro blues singer who has cropped up
in recent years, Robert Johnson. Recording them in deepest Mississippi, Vocalion has certainly done right by us in
the tunes 'Last Fair Deal Gone Down' and 'Terraplane Blues'
to mention only two of the four sides already released, sung
to his own guitar accompaniment. Johnson makes Leadbelly sound like an accomplished poseur."[2]

    The notice launched three themes that would be re-
peated in criticism of Johnson's work and attempts to construct his biography for the rest of the century. First, the

notice contained a factual error—in this case, the location of Johnson's recording session. Second, the notice indicated that Johnson was somehow unique among blues artists, more authentic than even the better-known Leadbelly. And third, the notice contained strong hints that the northern literary establishment heard Johnson's music in a frame of reference that would have been alien to the artist's southern audience. Note, for example, that the song "Last Fair Deal Gone Down" was mentioned first, privileged perhaps because it was a composition based on a work song and contained the line "My captain's so mean to me," a reference that clearly dovetailed with the left-wing affinity for songs of social and political protest. On the other hand, "Terraplane Blues," with its risqué double entendre, was far more appealing to Johnson's African American audience in the South and was his biggest selling record.

It is particularly interesting that Johnson was compared to Leadbelly (Huddie Ledbetter), the only other down-home musician whose name was likely to ring a bell with many *New Masses* readers. Leadbelly had been released three years earlier from a Louisiana prison through the intercession of folklorists John and Alan Lomax, and by the late thirties he was closely associated with proletarian and leftist politics. The comparison to Leadbelly buttressed the columnist's contention that Robert Johnson was the "greatest Negro blues singer" to emerge in many years— after all, he made the old master sound like a phony by comparison. These two ideas—that Johnson was the greatest and that his voice was the most authentic—would carry first into the sixties, when Johnson was crowned the king of the Delta blues singers and the very sound of his recorded voice caused critics to experience panic attacks and other creepy feelings, and then into the seventies, eighties, and nineties, when Johnson, still the king of delta blues, was also declared an originator of rock and roll.

As to the factual error, it probably made Johnson's records more exotic to say they were made in "deepest Mississippi," which is, after all, a far piece from Manhattan and Brooklyn, but as the reader already knows, the sides were cut in San Antonio.

In the following issue of *New Masses*, the same two Johnson titles were mentioned again among recommended recordings. And in the June 8 issue, just days before the start of Johnson's final recording sessions in

Texas, a second extended reference was published, this time with the byline of John Hammond, who would become Johnson's initial promoter and a key informant in Johnson's early biography. The belief that John Hammond and Henry Johnson were one and the same rests on three pieces of evidence. First, the writing styles were similar. Second, the initials were the same, albeit transposed. And third, Hammond's middle name was Henry, making him the junior John Henry, John's son.

> There is not very much to grow excited about in the jazz world. Vocalion is doing some interesting recording in Birmingham, Ala., Hot Springs, Ark., and San Antonio, Tex. Alabama has produced a fairish band, known as Bogans Birmingham Busters, which is better than any I have ever encountered in Birmingham, while Hot Springs' star is still Robert Johnson, who has turned out to be a worker on a Robinsville, Miss. plantation. It's too bad that Vocalion, which is the only company that takes regular trips through the backwoods of the South, records no work songs or songs of protest by Negro artists.[3]

Once again the facts about Johnson were distorted. Vocalion had done sessions in Hot Springs, but not with Johnson. Hammond's belief to the contrary could have been formed after he listened to "32–20 Blues," the flip side of Johnson's "Last Fair Deal Gone Down," in which the Arkansas resort town is mentioned. Hammond evidently had not yet been in touch with Don Law and so was unaware that Johnson had done all his recording up to that point in San Antonio.

The Hammond mention in *The New Masses,* like the earlier mention, set out a perception of Johnson that seems to be influenced more by the writer's beliefs and preconceptions than by the reality of Johnson's life and art. Hammond's brief description of Johnson reflected an impression— soon to be reinforced by Don Law and Ernie Oertle—that Johnson was an unsophisticated plantation hand. This typecasting, which was consistent with the then-current understanding of what a "folk artist" should be, continued for decades, even though the rustic image stood in stark contrast to Johnson's real-life status as an up-to-date or even cutting-edge blues professional.

The complaint about Vocalion's choice of material also could be attributed to Hammond's folk orientation. But it is equally plausible that the complaint reflected Hammond's personal political views and the left-ist orientation of *The New Masses*.[4] If so, this would illustrate, again, the vastly different reference points white critics and African American record buyers applied to recorded blues. Work and protest songs were not what Johnson's down-home audience wanted to hear and thus not what Vocalion wanted to record. This disconnect—the biases, yearnings, and preconceptions of white writers, on one hand, and the cultural reference points of Johnson and his down-home audience, on the other—would dominate the discussions of Johnson's art for the rest of the century.

In addition to miscasting Johnson as a plantation worker, Hammond's brief review put the plantation in "Robinsville," a truncated version of *Robinsonville*. Like the miscasting, the mangled name took on a life of its own, showing up along the paper trail for decades.

Hammond's (and Henry Johnson's) effervescent responses to John-son's playing and singing would be echoed for decades, one early example being found in *The Jazz Record Book*, a critical overview of available recordings published in 1942. The book offered a brief commentary on Johnson's top-selling record, "Terraplane Blues" backed by "Kindhearted Woman Blues."[5] It reported, erroneously, that Johnson had been "trained by an old time New Orleans guitar player,"[6] said the guitar playing on the record was "as exciting as almost any in the folk blues field," and described Johnson's singing as "imaginative" and "thrilling." Once again, we see the New York City jazz establishment portraying Johnson as a "folk blues" artist and responding enthusiastically to his musicianship.

While the authors appreciated Johnson's hit record, they deemed it important to mention the protest and work-song qualities of "Last Fair Deal Gone Down," which they described as "the story of a job, a mean 'cap'n' and a railroad construction gang." Here we see a possible reflection of the leftist liberal aesthetic of fellow New Yorkers Hammond and Moe Asch, the founder of Folkways Records, which employed two of *The Jazz Record Book*'s authors, Charles Edward Smith and Frederick Ramsey Jr.

Finally, the commentary on Johnson came in a subsection of the book's chapter on blues and boogie-woogie titled "Long, Long Way from Home." The title emphasized the distance between the New York jazz scene and the artists, such as Johnson, who played folk blues (or "bottom blues")—music the Eastern jazz critics of that day tended to perceive as strange and exotic, evocative of another place and an earlier time.

❁

In 1946, eight years after Johnson's death, the jazz critic Rudi Blesh chose a single Johnson recording, "Hellhound on My Trail," to review in his book *Shining Trumpets: A History of Jazz.* Blesh made this choice despite the fact that "Hellhound" is not at all representative of Johnson's style; it is more representative of Johnson's ability to assimilate and mimic the styles of other artists, in this case, that of his fellow Mississippi blues artist Skip James, as heard in James's 1931 recording "Devil Got My Woman."

Blesh, a Berkeley-educated designer and jazz buff whose childhood musical training had been classical, also initiated a methodological approach that was a sure-fire recipe for disaster. He tried to create Johnson from the "Hellhound" song text, suggesting that Johnson was so haunted, so consumed, by supernatural feelings that he was virtually speaking (or singing) in tongues. Or so it seemed to Blesh, who found Johnson's vocal articulation, "like speech in possession," difficult to understand. Blesh then launched into a lyrical description of Johnson's "Hellhound" performance:

> The images—the wanderer's voice and its echoes, the mocking wind running through the guitar strings, and the implacable, slow, pursuing footsteps—are full of evil, surcharged with the terror of one alone among the moving, unseen shapes of the night. Wildly and terribly, the notes paint a dark wasteland, starless, ululant with bitter wind, swept by the chill rain. Over a hilltop trudges a lonely, ragged, bedeviled figure, bent to the wind, with his *easy rider* held by one arm as it swings from its cord around his neck.[7]

Years later, the blues researcher and author Peter Guralnick said Blesh's lurid passage came close to capturing the "breathless rush of feeling" and "sense of awe" he and his friends experienced the first time they heard Robert Johnson's recordings.[8] Blesh's images were breathless, no doubt about that. But they were also absurdly out of context, illustrating the pitfalls that awaited any outsider who tried to interpret the oral tradition of a southern regional artist.

Blesh's transcriptions of the "Hellhound" lyrics show that he did indeed have trouble with Johnson's articulation, but his mistakes in this regard were minor, especially compared to later efforts by other writers. Blesh's flawed methodology was more significant for two other reasons besides the transcription difficulties and the unfortunate selection of "Hellhound" to represent Johnson. First, it led Blesh to miss all the song's underlying themes; second, he attributed feelings and images to Johnson that were pure inventions, unsupported by anything in the song lyrics. In both regards Blesh set patterns other writers would follow.

Blesh also added a second key component to the early miscasting of Johnson. Johnson was now a country folk artist who was haunted by the supernatural.

Blesh and Hammond epitomized forces behind what now seems like a vast divide in the way Johnson's music was perceived. On one side of the divide were the consumers, mostly African Americans living mainly in the South, who bought Johnson's records (though not very many of them) and turned out at rural jooks or urban clubs to hear him play in person. On the other side were the critics, collectors, and musicians, comparatively few in number and predominantly white, who came to Johnson's music from a jazz orientation and never heard him play in person. To African American record buyers, Johnson and the other regional blues artists of his era were entertainers, representatives of popular culture, part of a vibrant, ongoing musical tradition. To the jazz critics, however, artists such as Johnson, Blind Lemon Jefferson, and Big Bill Broonzy were living museum pieces, exemplars of an older blues style—Blesh termed it "archaic"[9]—that had been one of the original ingredients in the musical gumbo that became known as jazz. Blesh, to illustrate, believed that blues, spirituals, work songs, and other forms of African American "folk" expression had come together in New Orleans in an "extraordinary concatenation" of cultural and historical circumstances that occurred during the decades between the end of the Civil War and the start of the twentieth century, a miraculous, one-time synthesis from which jazz supposedly emerged.[10] Hammond, too, perceived the blues of such artists as Johnson and Broonzy, who played in Johnson's stead at the 1938 "From

Spirituals to Swing" concert, as "primitive" antecedents of jazz. One of Hammond's stated purposes in organizing the New York concert was to give "sophisticated jazz fans" a chance, at last, to hear "the sources of their music."[11] Hammond would almost certainly have been surprised to learn that Johnson had worked in both rural and urban venues, from Friars Point to St. Louis to Brooklyn, and that he had easily handled requests for many of the popular songs and swing tunes of his day, not just blues. At that time such conscious artistry would have detracted from Johnson's value as an authentic folk artist whose blues, along with those of Leadbelly, Blind Lemon, and Broonzy, helped to explain the genesis of jazz and popular music. The perceptions of Hammond, Blesh, and other jazz buffs had the effect of pushing blues back in time, distancing it from contemporary music and from living African American communities, recasting it as folk art, and leading inevitably to pronouncements that authentic (read: "archaic") blues had died out. To be fair, blues scholarship barely existed at that time, and jazz scholarship was in its infancy. The history of blues as perceived by jazz critics such as Blesh and Hammond would undergo a dramatic reassessment starting around 1959, as the reissue of scores of previously unknown recordings from the twenties and thirties began to make it abundantly clear that southern regional blues had been a dynamic, continuously evolving art form throughout the period when it was being pronounced dead. Despite this reassessment, however, the early jazz critics greatly influenced the methodology that would be applied to blues and to Johnson for much of the twentieth century. In essence, the original dichotomy would remain undisturbed: on one side, the African Americans who maintained the blues tradition; on the other side, the white spectators interested mainly in appropriating the tradition for their own uses, including scholars who used African Americans to explain blues or who used blues to explain African Americans.

In 1959 the record producer Samuel B. Charters, another writer who came to blues from a jazz background, published what was probably the most influential blues-related book of its time, *The Country Blues*. In it Charters made an important distinction between the aesthetic preferences of Johnson's down-home audience and those of later Eurocentric, literary-based critics. But Charters, who wanted to interest a small but growing blues-revival audience in the work of traditional country artists, fell victim to the same kind of farfetched interpretation that had marked the writing of Blesh. In a five-page section of the book focusing on Johnson, Charters wrote: "His singing becomes so disturbed it is almost impossible to understand the words. The voice and the guitar rush in an incessant rhythm. As he sings he seems to cry out in a high falsetto voice. Johnson seemed emotionally disturbed by the image of the devil, the 'Hellhound,' and he used the image in at least two blues. His last group of recordings included 'Hellhound on My Trail' and 'Me and the Devil Blues.' The figure seems to be his torment." [12]

Like Blesh, Charters was trying to inform readers about a blues singer whose words and meanings he had difficulty understanding. His solution was to psychoanalyze Johnson by interpreting what he thought he understood in specific song texts. Thus he cited Johnson's only two recorded blues containing devil or hellhound references to establish that the artist was deeply troubled by some sort of personal aberration. The critic-as-psychoanalyst approach was noteworthy because it was duplicated and expanded by later writers.

The Country Blues also reported three other tidbits of information about Johnson: First, there was an unattributed anecdote that told of Johnson recording in a San Antonio pool hall where a fight broke out, during which someone hurled a billiard ball and smashed several record masters. "The company ledger sheets for the recordings November 23, 26 and 27, 1936, list only a single recording," Charters deduced, possibly on the basis of incomplete information, "so the story may be true." [13] It wasn't. The anecdote was one of the few to be ignored in early biographies of Johnson.

Charters also cited a 1941 Alan Lomax interview with Muddy Waters in which Waters said he knew of Johnson but never saw him perform. In later years, as researchers persistently tried to establish some connection, Waters edged closer to saying he had actually seen Johnson, or at least someone who looked like Johnson. Persistence paid off in 1970 when the jazz and blues writer Pete Welding quoted Waters as saying, "I did get to see Robert play a few times, but I was digging his records, too."

Finally, Charters reported that the Memphis Jug Band leader Will Shade recalled once playing with Johnson in a band format in West Memphis. The Shade recollection becomes significant because it fits with other reports that Johnson enjoyed sitting in with bands or small combos. The musicians with whom he worked over the course of his short career included Johnny Shines, Johnny Temple, Floyd Jones, Elmore James, Sonny Boy Williamson no. 2, Willie Moore, and Henry Townsend. Townsend, who played guitar and piano, said Johnson was easy to accompany because he had "regular time" and would cue the other musicians.[14]

As a street musician, though, Johnson much preferred to work solo. Evidence suggests that his reasons for doing so were entirely practical: He had developed a style of finger-picking that mimicked the separate right- and left-hand functions heard in blues piano, so he didn't need the support of another guitar player,[15] and Johnson figured he could make more money solo. As Shines recalled it, Johnson once told him: "You play on that corner and I'll play on this corner. If we play together and get twenty-five cents, that's only twelve and a half cents apiece. But if you make a quarter and I make a quarter, that's twenty-five cents apiece."[16]

✻

While Johnson often worked solo and concealed his chords and fingering from other musicians, he was willing to share his musical knowledge once he was away from the competitive spotlight. Robert "Junior" Lockwood, whose mother was one of only two or three women who had long-term relationships with Johnson, said Johnson taught him how to play guitar, helping him begin career as a blues musician. Arkansas-born Floyd Jones, one of Johnson's contemporaries, recalled a house party where Johnson played; after the crowd left, Jones said, Johnson gave him some pointers on playing slide guitar: "He told me quite a few things."[17] Henry Townsend said Johnson often seemed to assume that other musicians would "automatically" know how to play certain things. "But on the other hand," Townsend said, "if he found that you didn't know, why, he had enough patience to take time out and show you."[18]

It will be instructive to keep these and other similar recollections in mind as we review the literature from the sixties and seventies and see Johnson increasingly portrayed as a singular artist and pathological loner who shunned the company of other people.

5   The Reissue Project, Phase One

The stuff I got'll bust your brains out, baby. . . it'll make you lose your mind.
  —Robert Johnson, "Stop Breakin' Down Blues" (1937)

The Johnson legend was greatly influenced by Columbia's two-stage reissue of the artist's recordings in 1961 and 1970. The first of these two albums, *King of the Delta Blues Singers* (CL 1654), was released during a wave of popular interest in American folk music. The folk revival, as it was called, started in the late fifties and peaked in the early sixties, bringing new recognition and in some cases new careers to dozens of artists who performed old-time music, including a number of "rediscovered" blues artists from the twenties and thirties. Spurred by the revival, the acoustic guitar became the instrument of choice for the counterculture generation that came of age in the sixties. The word *hootenanny* entered the popular lexicon. Millions of middle-class Americans sang ballads, blues, and other traditional songs at parties, coffeehouses, festivals, concerts, and rallies. It is no surprise, then, that Robert Johnson was marketed as a folk blues artist in the counterculture mold. The first reissue album emphasized the artist's image as an outsider, a mysterious loner driven by dark fears and anxieties—an image that was reflected in the album's cover, the choice of cuts, and the liner notes.

The cover featured Burt Goldblatt's stylized painting of a lone guitarist as seen from above, seated in a chair, head averted, and staring down at his guitar. The figure is balanced by its shadow, producing a dualism between physical and shadowy presence and an effect of solitude.

The album began with "Cross Road Blues" and ended with "Hellhound on My Trail." The fourteen cuts in between included "If I Had Possession over Judgment Day," "Preaching Blues," and "Me and the Devil Blues." The titles conjured images of religion and the supernatural and supported the perception of Johnson as an artist who was troubled by psychological demons. The song selection, particularly the first and final cuts, also supplied fodder for the Faustian story line that would soon be linked to Johnson. Almost as telling was what Columbia left off the reissue. The missing cuts included "Sweet Home Chicago" and "Dust My Broom," traditional pieces that would have connected Johnson to the rightful inheritors of his musical ideas—big-city African American artists whose high-powered, electrically amplified blues remained solidly in touch with Johnson's musical legacy.

The album's producer and editor was Frank Driggs, a jazz promoter who at one time was said to have the world's most extensive collection of jazz-related photos and memorabilia. According to most sources, John H. Hammond Jr., who was then an executive at Columbia Records, also had a hand in producing the album as part of the label's Thesaurus of Classic Jazz series. While Hammond still believed that Johnson's music exemplified the "primitive" origins of jazz, there was no hint of that view in the album's liner notes. The notes, written by Driggs, introduced the blues artist this way: "Robert Johnson is little, very little more than a name on aging index cards and a few dusty master records in the files of a phonograph company that no longer exists. A country blues singer from the Mississippi Delta that brought forth Son House, Charlie Patton, Bukka White, Muddy Waters and John Lee Hooker, Robert Johnson appeared and disappeared, in much the same fashion as a sheet of newspaper twisting and twirling down a dark and windy midnight street."

Visually evocative but uninformative, Driggs's fervid prose dehumanized Johnson and underscored the man-of-mystery theme. The liner notes passed along a few choice bits from Samuel Charters's book *The Country Blues* but omitted the pool-hall recording anecdote. Driggs, who had spoken to Don Law, the producer of Johnson's recording sessions in the thirties, recounted Law's impressions of Johnson—that he was fresh off the plantation, painfully shy, and so on—and retold the Law anecdotes about Johnson, including the legend of the Mexican musicians. Having exhausted what then passed for biographical data, Driggs resorted to the standard procedure of analyzing song lyrics to construct a picture of Johnson. Driggs's impressions of Johnson included the following: "He seemed constantly trapped," "He was tormented by phantoms and weird, threatening monsters," and "Symbolic beasts seemed to give him a great deal of trouble." In one particularly inventive burst, sparked by verses from "Kindhearted Woman Blues" and "Walkin' Blues," Driggs told his readers: "With a fairly large bank roll for that time and place, naïve Johnson was probably fair game for smart connivers. More than one sank her claws into Johnson, only to ditch him when the money ran out." Based on the testimony of his peers, though, it was more often Johnson who was doing the conniving and the ditching. Johnny Shines, for one, said Johnson used women the way most people use hotel rooms—a short stay and then gone, a pattern that was not uncommon among walking musicians in that era.[1] Driggs, like others before him, had read too much into lyrics he was ill-equipped to understand.

To be fair, the liner notes, for all their excesses, were better than average for that era, and the writer's belief that blues lyrics were autobiographical was once a commonly held assumption outside African American culture. Even giving Driggs his due, however, we can now see that the liner notes to this extremely influential album, along with the selection and sequence of songs and the moody cover illustration, helped to entrench the image of Johnson as an obscure, tormented loner whose most revealing songs were "Hellhound," "Cross Road Blues," and "Me and the Devil."

Driggs also continued a pattern of recycling information about Johnson without checking or challenging it. In addition to relating the standard canon of anecdotes, legends, and impressions, for example, the notes contained a reference to the "plantation in Robinsville, Mississippi" where Johnson supposedly was raised—a repetition of the mistake that first appeared in the June 1937 issue of *New Masses*. (The "Robins-ville" spelling surfaced most recently in Sherman Alexie's novel *Reserva-tion Blues* in 1996.)

As Blesh, Charters, and Driggs demonstrated, the problem of understand-ing Johnson's words and then interpreting them in print presented a for-midable challenge. It was complicated, as Charters well knew, by the enormous cultural gulf between the predominantly white critics who conducted the postmortem examinations of Johnson's music and the African American consumers who bought Johnson's records and gath-ered at local jook joints to hear him play. To down-home audiences the raw intensity of Johnson's singing—what other blues musicians referred to simply as "feeling"—was entertaining, even moving, but also comfort-ably familiar: a style of artistic expression deeply rooted in rural African American culture. Probably because the Eurocentric critics and review-ers lacked a similarly comfortable frame of reference, they were aston-ished by Johnson's "feeling," and their subsequent reactions soared into the romantic red zone. Here's a section from a 1966 Pete Welding essay titled "Hell Hound on His Trail: Robert Johnson": "To hear Johnson was to believe him immediately, to join him in his private world of misery, to travel with him along the byroads of despair and anxiety and rejection that were the sole markers of his demon-driven journey through life, a life that was all too quickly burned out in dissipations and finally death by poisoning."[2]

Welding's passage did suggest one valid aesthetic point, namely, that in the world of the blues, the audience wants to believe that the artist actually feels whatever he's singing about. Welding went too far, howev-er, projecting his own feelings into Johnson's singing. In a 1971 reissue of the essay, Welding owned up to his zeal, describing the previous pas-sage as "vintage rococo Welding"[3]—almost as if to say, "Jeez, what got into me that day?" But rococo was the rule rather than the exception when-ever writers tried to come to grips with Johnson.

The 1966 Welding essay was significant for another, more ominous reason: It formally launched the notion that Johnson was a twentieth-century incarnation of the legendary Faust, a sixteenth-century astrologer who supposedly sold his soul to the devil to gain knowledge and magical power and who thus incurred God's anger. The Welding piece quoted Son House, one of Johnson's early musical mentors, as saying that Johnson might have bartered his soul to the devil to acquire talent as a blues musician. The reference was brief and more than a little dubious, as we will show later. But over the next three decades, this story line would prove to be irresistible. It would be expanded and embellished. It would be gussied up with quasi-scholarly research and language. Eventually it would become the core of the Robert Johnson legend.

☼

In 1965, with the publication of Paul Oliver's work *Conversations with the Blues,* we begin to see the first inklings of a potential biographical reassessment. Based on his "conversations" with Robert "Junior" Lockwood and Sunnyland Slim, Oliver was struck by the difference between the impressions Johnson made on his fellow musicians and the representation handed down by Don Law et al. and embellished by Blesh, Charters, Driggs, and Welding. Instead of recalling Johnson as a shy teenage singer who spent most of his life on a plantation and whose music represented the culmination of the old folk styles, fellow musicians painted a picture of a restless, widely influential, and charismatic young artist whose singing and instrumental styles precipitated modern trends in blues.[4] Alas, despite these insights, Oliver concluded that Robert Johnson remained "something of a mystery." And four years later, in his book *The Story of the Blues,* Oliver, too, fell under Johnson's demonic spell. Extending a trend started by Charters and Driggs, Oliver resorted to overblown psychoanalysis based on hearsay that Johnson had one bad eye in an apparent attempt to solve the Johnson mystery: "Perhaps Johnson's defective eye caused him to feel the need to assert himself with women, and he may have been somewhat paranoiac; whether he was or not, his blues, with the hard, angry utterances and the obsessional nature of many of his themes undoubtedly suggest it."[5]

To underscore the point, Oliver offered lyrics from "Me and the Devil Blues" as evidence of Johnson's "obsessional" character and his insecurity about the "defective eye."[6] In the lyrics of "Hellhound on My Trail" and "If I Had Possession over Judgment Day," Oliver professed to find "evidence of a tormented spirit."

If there was going to be a sober reassessment of Johnson's life, it would have to wait.

6   Reissue, Phase Two

> If Robert Johnson had not existed, they would have to have
> invented him."
>
> —Bruce Cook, *Listen to the Blues*

The second installment of Columbia's vinyl reissue series
showed a significant shift. It was now 1970, the popularity
of traditional folk music had waned, the Beatles and other British groups had pumped new life into the rock move-
ment, and Robert Johnson was being recast as an inventor of rock and roll. In an introduction on the back of the
second album's cover, Jon Waxman, a Columbia marketing
manager who had been under contract to the label as a
rock musician when still in his teens, wrote: "As rock has
gradually begun to incorporate new elements from other
music forms, both musicians and listeners alike seem to
have developed a new interest in its roots. Unquestionably,
a major influence on much of today's rock music is the
blues—more specifically rural blues. . . . So, if you dig contemporary music, especially the blues, give a listen to Robert Johnson, the original master."[1]

Note that Waxman tied rock and roll to rural blues rather
than to rock's more immediate predecessor, urban rhythm
and blues. The fact that the Rolling Stones and Eric Clapton had recorded Johnson's songs (Waxman specifically

mentioned the Stones' version of "Love in Vain") was an early sign that rock musicians, particularly in the United Kingdom, were embracing Johnson and other blues artists as musical ancestors who could lend depth, legitimacy, and even a touch of mystique to rock's family tree.[2] And of course, the association could work the other way, too: Linking modern rockers to Johnson's music could help drive sales of the second reissue album.

Despite this new marketing tack, Pete Welding's liner notes, packaged inside the record jacket, returned to the tenor of the initial reissue album. Resurrecting many of the images and descriptions first published in his 1966 essay about Johnson in *Down Beat* magazine, Welding portrayed Johnson not as one of the fathers of contemporary rock but as a singular artist whose music reflected an outlook of unimaginable bleakness: "No other blues are so apocalyptic in their life view. They are shot through with dark foreboding, and almost total disenchantment with the human condition."

Welding said Johnson's songs focused on three recurrent themes: the impermanence of human relations, incessant wandering, and the "besetting, mindless terrors that haunted all his days and nights." The first two themes were right on. The third was yet another flight of fancy. Unfortunately Welding didn't stop there: "His songs are the diary of a wanderer through the tangle of the black underworld, the chronicle of a sensitive black Orpheus in his journey along the labyrinthine path of the human psyche. In his songs one hears the impassioned, unheeded cries of man, rootless and purposeless. The acrid stench of evil burns ever in his mind."[3]

This is absolutely riveting stuff. You can almost hear its cadences being shouted by a down-home holy roller preacher. But it has no relevance to Robert Johnson's blues, as we will try to demonstrate in later chapters.

Welding's notes described Johnson as a tireless perfectionist who would practice a song as many times as necessary to get it exactly the way he wanted it. Having perfected a song, Welding wrote, Johnson would always perform it that way without any noticeable deviation. Welding claimed that this observation was corroborated by the alternative takes of Johnson's recorded songs and the testimony of Johnson's peers.

There is peer testimony concerning Johnson's willingness to rehearse with an accompanist before a gig, but it is difficult to find support for

Welding's portrayal of Johnson as a musician who spent vast amounts of time perfecting his songs. Johnny Shines said that in the time he spent with Johnson between 1933 or 1934 and 1938, he never saw Johnson sit down and learn a song and never saw him practice, noting that Johnson seemed to know how to play whatever song came into his mind.[4] The Shines account and the Welding account don't necessarily contradict each other, however; what Shines said he observed, for example, could have been the result of a process like the one described by Welding.

The supposed uniformity of Johnson's song presentations cannot be corroborated through his recordings, since the alternative takes do contain small and sometimes significant differences from the issued takes— a topic that we will revisit when we examine "Cross Road Blues" in chapter 11. Nor does the testimony of peers support the uniformity thesis. Henry Townsend, a St. Louis musician who worked with Johnson, said Johnson could modify the songs in his repertoire, using "several methods . . . in playing the same set of lyrics." In addition, Townsend said Johnson often seemed to improvise—pulling a song "out of nowhere"—when the mood struck him. Townsend made these observations in 1967 while being interviewed by Welding.[5]

Welding ended his notes with several accounts of Johnson's death. It could have been a merciful ending, but like so many before him, Welding couldn't resist touching up the death scene with a bit of personal adornment: "However apocryphal the accounts, they have one thing in common: all detail an end for a man who all through his adult years felt the hounds of hell baying loudly and relentlessly on his trail. In the end, he just couldn't outrun them any longer."

All this is gleaned from one song, "Hellhound on My Trail," and one critic's need to find a supernatural thread with which to stitch up an essay. Or perhaps we're reading too much into Welding's prose. After all, Johnny Shines said he heard that Johnson died on his hands and knees, barking like a dog, whereas Honeyboy Edwards said the mortally poisoned Johnson was retching with dry heaves. Perhaps it's just a difference of language and imagery: puking like a dog or "baying loudly and relentlessly" like hounds from hell.

✿

The year after Columbia released its second reissue album, *Rolling Stone* magazine published a short piece on Johnson, mentioning the two reissue albums but avoiding the second album's suggestion of a direct link between Johnson's music and contemporary rock and roll. The piece portrayed Johnson as an artist whose life was shrouded in mystery and whose brand of blues was the product of a certain time and place in the rural South, asserting "we know we will never see it again."[6]

That same year Peter Guralnick, who would later become Johnson's best-known biographer, published *Feel Like Going Home: Portraits in Blues and Rock n Roll.* He argued in favor of Johnson's place in the evolution of rock and roll—pointing to the influence of Johnson's music on Muddy Waters, who in turn became an inspiration for the Rolling Stones and other sixties groups—and he perpetuated the image of Johnson as an artist in anguish: "Robert Johnson fulfilled in every way the requisite qualities of the blues myth. Doomed, haunted, dead at an early age; desperate, driven, a brief flickering of tormented genius. Not one of his songs fails to bear out these romantic associations."[7]

As proof Guralnick offered the first verse of "Hellhound," the first two verses of "Me and the Devil Blues," and the first verse of "Stones in My Passway." Hardly a sufficient sample to support the sweeping assertion that all Johnson's songs laid bare the inner turmoil of a demonized genius. Still, although Guralnick was guilty of gross overstatement, he had plenty of company.

In his 1973 book *Listen to the Blues,* Bruce Cook attempted to explain Johnson's importance this way: "If Robert Johnson had not existed, they would have to have invented him. He is the most potent legend in all the blues—that of the gifted young artist, driven by his hunger for life and his passion for music to excesses that killed him at the age of twenty-four. . . . He is the Shelley, Keats, and Rimbaud of the blues all rolled into one. If any bluesman is assured of immortality it is this little drifter-with-a-guitar who may never have left the South."[8]

Cook would have been closer to the mark if he had written that even though Robert Johnson *had* existed, successive waves of critics and researchers still invented and reinvented him, too often in their own images. Although Cook obviously erred on Johnson's age at death, keep in mind that Johnson was widely believed, even by his musical contemporaries, to be somewhat younger than he was, and his death certificate, discovered the same year that Cook's book was published, listed the artist as being younger (twenty-six) than he was—assuming that the most commonly accepted date of birth is accurate. As for the statement that Johnson "may never have left the South," Cook had interviewed Johnny Shines, so presumably he should have found out that Shines and Johnson traveled together as far north as Ontario, Canada.

In 1973 Samuel Charters returned to the fray with *Robert Johnson,* a short work detailing Johnson's recorded blues, preceded by an introduction that attempted to place the songs in a biographical context. The introduction drew primarily on interviews with Son House, Johnny Shines, Muddy Waters, Honeyboy Edwards, Henry Townsend, and Robert "Junior" Lockwood. Even Don Law was revisited. Although the sources for the interview material were not always clear, the essay was informative—except for a renewed effort to establish that Johnson and his music were "haunted" by relentless, dark images. Picking up where he had left off fourteen years earlier in *The Country Blues,* Charters cited the obligatory verses from "Me and the Devil Blues" and "Hellhound on My Trail" and asserted: "In six of his blues he mentions the devil or the supernatural—voodoo, and it seemed to force its presence on some of his greatest music."[9]

Not that it makes any difference, but we count only four blues containing such references.[10] On the other hand, the respected Memphis-based scholar David Evans, to whom we will return later, finds direct and indirect references to sorcery, voodoo, Satan, and the supernatural in a majority of Johnson blues. Determining the exact number of references, though, is a distraction from the main point: Supernatural themes haunted not Johnson's music itself but *discussions* of Johnson's music. It is apparent that each successive wave of critics became obsessed with two songs and analyzed them to a fare-thee-well while largely ignoring the artist's major contribution to the blues tradition.

Charters ventured even deeper into the supernatural waters by suggesting—perhaps unwittingly—that Johnson had been mixed up in a deal with the devil. He did this first with an oft-cited quotation from Son House recalling how quickly Johnson seemed to progress from novice musician to virtuoso. As House told the story, young Johnson was a mediocre guitar player who used to sneak out of his family's house and show up at parties around Robinsonville whenever House and his sidekick Willie Brown were providing the music. Eventually, House said, Johnson ran away from home to escape the drudgery of farmwork and the tyranny of his stepfather. When he returned, just six months later, House recalled, he could play faster and better than either of his two former mentors— and proved it by showing them up at one of their own gigs.

As told by House, it was a highly entertaining story.[11] Charters felt it was credible enough to say that "the essential outline . . . must be true." However, the essential outline has been weakened considerably by information that has come to light since the publication of Charters's book. It is now believed, for example, that before he left Robinsonville Johnson was already a better musician than House recalled, since there are reports of Johnson performing professionally during the time of his first marriage. And Johnson's absence from Robinsonville was certainly longer than House recalled. It was at least a year or two, possibly more; in fact, some researchers theorize that the encounter with House and Brown could have occurred shortly before Johnson's death. Even so, the House account has always commanded special consideration precisely because the speaker's time-compressed recollections—in which Johnson learned guitar in "about six months"—meshed so neatly with the folk belief that overnight prowess as a secular musician was a sure sign of a bargain with Satan or some other supernatural agent. Keep in mind that House never actually mentioned Satan in this version of his colorful recollection, never even hinted at an unholy bargain as far as we know. Yet his story became grist for latter-day writers and record hucksters invested in the "Hellhound" version of the Robert Johnson story. Should we thus include Charters among the "Hellhound" conspirators? Probably not. To see why, let us return to his 1973 book.

Having reported House's story about Johnson, Charters then brought in a quote from Johnny Shines, who said he remembered how hard he had once tried to emulate the playing of Howling Wolf, even though common wisdom said "a guy that played like Wolf, he'd sold his soul to the devil." What emerged from the proximity of the House and Shines quotes was a kind of guilt by association—with Johnson's learning guitar seemingly overnight tied to Shines's talk about a deal with the devil—and Charters seemed to be driving the point home when he wrote in summation,

"What Son remembers with Robert is so close to what Johnny remembers with Howling Wolf that it must be true."[12]

But what was "it"? A close reading of the Charters text suggests that "it" had nothing to do with soul-selling. Charters wove the colorful quotations and recollections into a discussion of an old ritual: the moment when a blues protégé realizes he has surpassed his mentor and publicly proclaims his prowess by stealing the teacher's thunder in a public performance. That was the "it." But the occasional imprecision of Charters's writing, his assertion that supernatural images forced their presence on Johnson's music, and his proclivity for imaginative reveries about things Johnson might have done or seen in various places or situations opened a wide boulevard of interpretive latitude for blues fans and researchers seeking underpinnings for the growing Johnson legend. Was Charters guilty in this instance of willfully promulgating romanticized fiction about our hero? No reasonable jury would convict him.

Charters ended his introductory essay in enigmatic fashion, asserting that "the whole force of evil" permeated Johnson's "Hellhound on My Trail": "It's there as a theme, as so many things of his life became the themes of his music. Which of the themes was his life? All of them, and in that is the greatness of what he created."[13] Is this portentous or just pretentious? Charters seemed to be saying that Johnson lived the life about which he sang and sang about the life he lived, and that's what made his music so extraordinary. But there is little evidence to support such an equation between Johnson's art and Johnson's life, except in the romantic imaginings of latter-day critics.

In the end Charters's two main contentions—that Johnson's music was haunted by the supernatural and that all Johnson's themes were autobiographical—turned out to be romantic distortions. Johnson's repertoire, including his two most famous songs, was firmly grounded in blues tradition. No one knew that better than the artists whose interviews were used by Charters in his book on Johnson. They would have scoffed at Charters's blustery generalizations about satanic imagery and the presence of evil in Johnson's life and music.

It is always possible, of course, that some of Johnson's life experiences did filter into his lyrics. According to David Evans, however, there is no reason to suppose, as so many Johnson researchers do, that such songs as "Me and the Devil Blues" reflected what the artist actually did or felt: "Blues singers don't always create songs out of autobiographical incidents. It could have been a friend of his. It could have been just his imagination on a common folk theme that he put himself into. It could be just his imagination as an artist."[14] Most of Johnson's critics would let their own imaginations run wild in concocting stories about the artist's life and personality, but they were seldom willing to concede that the artist's own imagination could have been the source of the vivid images that illuminate his songs.

In 1975 rock critic Greil Marcus presented yet another imaginative portrait of Johnson in his highly influential *Mystery Train: Images of America in Rock and Roll Music.* In Johnson's song texts Marcus found images of demons, desolation, and shattered dreams, and in Johnson's music he professed to hear a "whole new aesthetic . . . a loud, piercing music driven by massive rhythms."[15] While this brand of music might well mark Johnson as the "first rock 'n' roller of all," Marcus argued that Johnson's strongest influence on contemporary music could be heard not in the covers of his songs recorded by rock groups but in the passion of such artists as Eric Clapton, Bob Dylan, and Randy Newman.

Johnson's potent song texts provided Marcus with ample fuel for his portrait of a tormented, bedeviled artist—a portrait we'll examine in chapter 12—except that Marcus suffered from the same interpretive problem that had hindered Blesh in 1946 and Charters in 1959: He couldn't understand the words. Unlike Blesh and Charters, however, Marcus admitted to no such problem and proceeded to analyze Johnson's poetic images based on what he confidently believed he heard. What sort of images? Here's one: In listening to Johnson's "Walkin' Blues," Marcus heard the name Bernice as *bunny ears.*[16] Never mind that *bunny ears* is wildly out of context. Never mind that the phrase would have stopped one of Johnson's jook joint audiences in its tracks: "What did he say?" "What did he call her?" The implausibility of the reference was not enough to shake the author's belief that what he (mis)heard was evidence of Johnson's whimsical humor. So now we have Johnson as a country folk artist who was haunted by a relationship with supernatural forces—possibly even the devil himself—but who was blessed with a quirky, humorous side.

Giles Oakley's book *The Devil's Music: A History of the Blues* (1976) would appear likely, based on title alone, to embellish the emerging Faust motif. Instead Oakley followed the tack taken earlier by Pete Welding and Paul Oliver, psychoanalyzing Johnson based on his song lyrics: "Taken together they create visions of a reckless, self destructive interior world filled with secret fears and anxieties. At times, he seems scarcely able to control the extremities of feeling which press in on him or the tensions and neuroses which drive, harry and confuse him. As if on the edge of an abyss of complete psychic disintegration his voice changes from high frenzy to little boy vulnerability." [17]

Is there any need to add that Oakley supports his diagnosis with the first verse of "Hellhound on My Trail"? In one variation from previous analyses, Oakley replaced the hounds of hell with up-to-date psychological parlance more familiar to modern listeners and critics. But his analysis, like others before it, had nothing to do with the song Johnson created.

Overall, the dark anxieties perceived by Oakley, Charters, Welding, and Oliver painted a pitiable picture of Johnson's mental health: The man was a wreck, a "paranoiac" and "tormented genius" embittered by "almost total disenchantment with the human condition" and driven by demons "along the byroads of despair and anxiety and rejection" to the very edge of "psychic disintegration." Could this be the same man whom a former girlfriend described as "loving and kind"? [18] Is this the man whom a friend and neighbor remembered as a "nice fellow" who liked people and was never "uppity or biggity"? [19] Is this the same Robert Johnson about whom Honeyboy Edwards said: "He was an awful friendly guy. He take with the public a whole lot—he played music in public and he liked to laugh and talk and drink. . . . He was a nice fellow. . . . You could get close to him. You always could talk to him. [20]

The St. Louis blues musician Henry Townsend offered a similar impression of Johnson in an interview with Welding: "I would say he was kind of an easygoing guy. . . . He was considerate. He wasn't sad or depressed—not that I could see. But this could have been an inward feeling that you only could tell from a song. You know, we all kind of have the tendency to unravel our inner feelings through this kind of thing. It could have been possible that Robert was like that, but he never did show it."[21]

Reading this remark, one gets the sense that Welding was fishing for testimony that would support his own portrait of Johnson as doomed and demon driven. Townsend's respectful response—maybe he felt depressed, but he never showed it—could have been an example of the way older blues musicians often deflected leading questions from white interviewers.[22] Whether it was or wasn't, the response nonetheless delicately disputed any dark suggestions from Welding about Johnson's psyche.

Overall the critics' view is so much at odds with the impressions of people who knew Johnson and who heard him perform that we have to challenge most, if not all, of the latter-day analyses. One begins to suspect that it is Robert who sits impassively in the chair, while Oakley, Charters, Welding, and company lie on the couch and pour out their obsessions.

When considering the agitated critical reaction to Johnson's recordings and all the psychiatric diagnoses pinned on our hero, it may be useful to remember that in live performance, blues artists are musical shrinks; they work for the positive mental health of the audience. One of Johnson's contemporaries, the late Roosevelt Sykes, explained it this way:

> Now some people don't understand. They think a blues player has to be worried, troubled to sing the blues. That's wrong; it's a talent. . . . So blues is sort of a thing on people like the doctor. I'll put it this way—there's a doctor; he has medicine; he's never sick; he ain't sick but he has stuff for the sick people. . . .
> "Call the doctor."
> "I'm the doctor."
> "Oh, you're a sick man."
> "No, I just work on the sick people."
> So the blues player, he ain't worried and bothered, but he got something for the worried people. Doctor: You can see his medicine; he can see his patient. Blues: You can't see the music; you can't see the patient, because it's soul. So I works on the soul and the doctor works on the body.[23]

While some artists may sing of their own experiences more than others, all artists know that audience response is best when a blues conveys feelings and experiences to which everyone can relate. When that happens, everyone in the club or jook joint or concert hall will be feeling good—often smiling or laughing—even if the shared experiences might seem painful or traumatic to a solitary critic listening to a recording of the same blues. This distinction seemed obvious to Ry Cooder, a white musician who wrote and played most of the score for the 1986 movie *Crossroads* and who consistently declined to be drawn into heavy-handed analyses of Johnson's records: "And what's not been recorded . . . is the little juke joint with [Johnson] and three other people. What that must've sounded like! And we wouldn't be having this conversation if we heard that, and that's the thing to remember: We'd know what the guy did. The stupid thing is to try to say, based on this brief moment of recording, 'Well, I therefore feel and think and conclude. . . .' Because every day of his life he did different things."[24]

By most accounts Johnson's best jook performances were everything Cooder might have imagined: audacious, bawdy, and artistically distinctive. But there were exceptions, according to musicians who knew Johnson. When Johnson drank too much, his artistry would sometimes take a backseat to womanizing, and his drunken rants at God could be vitriolic enough to frighten an audience into picking up and leaving. The indiscriminate womanizing was a particular worry to other musicians, because it had the potential to create serious trouble in a club or jook. Johnny Shines remembered getting "stomped" in more than one fight that erupted over something Johnson had said or done—or simply because Johnson, as a musician, had been attracting female attention.[25]

Shines also told a story about a place that he and Johnson played in St. Louis. During the gig, Shines said, Johnson took out a slide and went into a "very slow and passionate" rendition of "Come on in My Kitchen." The end of the song was followed by an unexpected quiet, Shines said, and it was only then that he noticed people—both men and women—were crying.[26]

The story told by Shines, however vivid a testimonial to Johnson's ability to move an audience, described an exceptional circumstance. In all other venues—jooks, street corners, parties—Johnson's music was intended to bring smiles, not tears. His songs, like most blues, focused on widely shared subjects to which his audiences could easily relate: changing towns, changing partners, seduction, betrayal, and sexual boasting. His playing was spirited, and his singing was loaded with sexual energy. What Giles Oakley heard as a voice change "from high frenzy to little boy vulnerability" was much more likely to be a strategy in a seduction song than a portent of psychic disintegration, as we will show in chapters 10 and 11. But that's the difference between listening to Johnson's songs in their natural setting and listening to his recordings on a set of headphones in the dead of night. Even today, if you hear a blues combo or a solo musician do "Dust My Broom" or "Sweet Home Chicago" or even "Come on in My Kitchen" in a bar or nightclub, the music will most often make you feel good, not sad or scared.

In 1982 Peter Guralnick published a new biography of Johnson. Titled *Searching for Robert Johnson,* the biography appeared first as a lengthy article in *Living Blues* magazine and was later republished as a short book. We will cite a couple of passages from the work in later chapters, but at this point we should note that it was the most thoroughly researched biography up to that time, and it remains the most well-known biography to this day.

Robert Palmer's *Deep Blues,* published in 1986, provided a thorough treatment of the Delta blues tradition from its Mississippi roots to the rise of rock. A popular, durable book, it featured a section on Johnson that, with the aid of Johnson's "Cross Road Blues," helped to cement the idea of a crossroads encounter between Johnson and the devil, the crossroads being a storied juncture between this world and the supernatural in both African and European folklore. Despite his knowledge of Delta traditions and his own experience as a musician, Palmer said he found "Hellhound on My Trail" and "Me and the Devil Blues" to be "chilling and apparently dead serious." More regrettable, Palmer fell victim to romantic license, imagining what Robert Johnson might have imagined at the fabled crossroads *if* he had been there late at night and *if* he had heard strange noises:

A friend who grew up in the Delta once told me of running out of gas late at night, walking several miles until he came to a deserted crossroads, hearing a far-off splashing, probably some animal crossing a creek or slough, and suddenly being seized with an unreasonable panic. He actually believed, before he got a grip on himself, that some sort of hideous swamp monster was lumbering toward him. Robert Johnson, alone in similar circumstances, might have imagined he was hearing the approach of Papa Legba, the Black Man.[27]

Palmer's imaginative stretch illustrates a political shift from the Eurocentric Satan to the Afrocentric Papa Legba, a shift that was amplified and extended by the expatriate blues artist Julio Finn in his 1986 book *The Bluesmen*. Reconstructing the Faust motif as a hoodoo initiation, Finn concluded that the mechanism for Johnson's art form was not Satan but the voodoo religion.[28] While this notion brought Johnson closer to his cultural roots, it also opened the door to Finn's imagination, allowing him to tell us what went on in Johnson's mind: "Looking out over the fields, he had visions of a world bathed in the light of peace. . . . At night, sweet voices came to him to whisper to him secret messages."[29] Once again, we find ourselves wondering how an author would know such things and questioning whose visions and whose inner voices are really being described.

In the same book Finn alluded to a dichotomy in the critical representations of Johnson, positing two opposing camps of biographers, "the bluesmen who knew him and believe he made a pact with the devil at the crossroads . . . and the folklorists, who don't."[30] Finn constructed this position, in part, on a belief that Son House, Johnny Shines, and Robert "Junior" Lockwood had always accepted the crossroads legend as true. As we have shown and will continue to show as this investigation moves along, however, it was always the scholarly writers who seemed most ready to promote the idea of a crossroads pact; House, Shines, and Lockwood were most often silent or skeptical on the question of a pact.

7 Myth Eclipses Reality

Robert was a nice-lookin man. Sort of brown skin. Sort of medium height, and got good hair.

—Muddy Waters, quoted in Paul Oliver, *Conversations with the Blues*

The first publication of a Johnson photograph came forty-eight years after the artist's death. The photo proved that Johnson's image could be recorded by conventional means, unlike, say, a vampire, whose body cannot be reflected in a mirror. More significantly, the photo showed that Johnson's face revealed no evidence of the anguish and inner torment that critics professed to hear in Johnson's music.

Rumors concerning the existence of Johnson photographs had circulated for years, and fans had become desperate for some likeness other than the drawings on Columbia's record jackets. The demand for a picture—any picture—was initially addressed in 1971 when *Living Blues,* America's first and foremost blues journal, commissioned a police artist to sketch a likeness of Johnson based on the recollections of two musicians who knew him, Eddie Taylor and Floyd Jones. A second drawing, based on the memory of Johnny Shines, also was published. The sketches, neither of which looked very human, served only to deepen the mystery and speculation about Johnson's appearance.[1]

In 1972 the blues researcher Mack McCormick supposedly located three photos. Two years later Stephen LaVere, the first researcher to gauge the Johnson mystique's full business potential, bought two of the photos from Johnson's sister.[2] Although some people were allowed to see the photos, neither was published until February 13, 1986, when the rock magazine *Rolling Stone* included a photo portrait of a youthful Robert Johnson, cigarette dangling from the left corner of his mouth, as part of an article on the opening of the Rock and Roll Hall of Fame and Museum in Cleveland. Johnson was one of three artists inducted that year in a special early-influence category.

So there it was, the first published photo of our hero. But it wasn't on the cover, which carried pictures of the hall's first ten rock and roll musician inductees (eleven if you count the Everly Brothers as two). The Johnson photo was buried on page 48, along with the other early-influence inductees, pianist Jimmy Yancy, blue yodeler Jimmie Rodgers, and two nonmusician inductees, disc jockey Alan Freed and record-company owner Sam Phillips. John H. Hammond Jr. was also inducted that year, honored for lifetime achievement. Arguably Hammond was also the person most responsible for Johnson's inclusion. But Hammond wasn't even mentioned in the magazine.[3]

The Hammond snub went largely unnoticed in the blues community, which was more miffed by what it saw as the cavalier treatment accorded Johnson. The Chicago writer Justin O'Brien criticized the magazine's iconoclasm in a *Living Blues* essay, grumbling that a culturally important photograph had been "handled casually, if not disrespectfully." The essay, however, was more significant for what it revealed about the way young fans had been affected by the overblown romanticism of material written about Johnson in the sixties and seventies. O'Brien specifically recalled the liner notes published as part of Columbia's reissue project: "My teenaged friends and I read and re-read the album notes, repeating the information to each other, marveling at the implications of the strange stories and haunting lyrics. Not knowing others with our interests, we became the cognoscenti, sharing a fascination in this mysterious man and equally mysterious music. It seemed it was ours to mythologize."

Even O'Brien, though, couldn't help but notice that the newly published photographic evidence of Johnson's human existence had the potential to destabilize the myth: "The serene, unblemished young face belies all the rumors of dark doings. It gives no suggestion of the obsessive fears and solitariness he felt and sang about."[4] Alas, the liner-note mythology proved too durable to surrender in the face of hard evidence; ultimately it was the rumored dark doings that overshadowed the serene photographic image.

The 1986 film *Crossroads* was the first pop-culture document to incorporate those dark doings. In it Johnson's art and the crossroads legend were fused in a fictional format aimed mainly at a rock-oriented youth market. The plot runs as follows: A boy (played by the youthful star Ralph Macchio) finds Johnson's long-lost mentor Willie Brown, still alive, in a New York hospital and learns that Brown once sold his soul to Papa Legba at the same crossroads where Johnson did. The boy gets Brown out of the hospital, travels to the Delta, and, with the help of Ry Cooder's sound track, beats Legba's representative in a guitar-playing contest at a jook joint. The boy then watches approvingly as Legba himself, seated in the audience, tears up the contract on Willie Brown's soul.

For longtime blues fans the best thing about the movie was the on-screen playing of Frank Frost, an honest-to-God Mississippi jook joint musician. For young newcomers to blues, however, the movie, although clearly fictional, may have lent new legitimacy to the notion that blues musicians of Robert Johnson's era were able to acquire talent through supernatural means. The researchers Gayle Dean Wardlow and Edward Komara later identified *Crossroads* as one of a half-dozen key building blocks in the construction of the Johnson legend.

During this same general time period, the Johnson photo portrait was reproduced in various formats. For example, it was used on a postage stamp—but minus the cigarette. Even the U.S. Postal Service felt free to touch up Johnson's image. The photo also served as the model for an R. Crumb drawing that graced the cover of an obscure music journal, *78 Quarterly*, in 1989. That issue of the journal (no. 4) published a second picture, the now-familiar posed photo of Johnson wearing a wide-lapel, pinstriped suit that belonged to a nephew who had entered the military. The journal announced that both photos were available as posters ("Dealer inquiries welcome").

Accompanying the photos in *78 Quarterly* was the second major body of research on Johnson's life, titled simply "Robert Johnson," by Stephen Calt and Gayle Wardlow. An objective and well-reasoned piece, it offered new detail and consistently refrained from the hysteria previously associated with the artist. As revisionist historians, the two authors distanced themselves from the legend by relying on the memories of the people who knew Johnson.

But 1989 also marked the publication of William Barlow's *Looking Up at Down: The Emergence of Blues Culture.* It included a brief section on Johnson, titled—as one might expect—"Robert Johnson: Hellhound on My Trail." With no apparent foundation, Barlow asserted that Johnson was "known to have encouraged the legend that he made a pact with Satan," which Barlow interpreted as "an extension of the fatalism implicit in his [Johnson's] philosophy." Barlow concluded: "It is important to note that the Devil is the ultimate trickster figure in Johnson's blues, a reincarnation of Legba at a Delta crossroads. Once again, cultural resistance is made manifest in the use of an African icon, here disguised as Satan, to reaffirm African custom and tradition."[5]

Like Julio Finn, Barlow opted for an Afrocentric reading of the devil deal, but by altering the pact with Satan from an act of personal gain to an act of cultural resistance, Barlow politicized the bargain. In this interpretation the morality play at the heart of the Johnson legend was no longer a warning to all sinners but rather a heroic tale of a cultural warrior using his art to fight the power structure. Barlow's view of Johnson, while inventive, was flawed on a number of counts. For openers, fatalism and cultural resistance seem to be incompatible concepts; Johnson was unlikely to embody both. For another thing, the idea that Johnson would consciously—or unconsciously—conceal within his song texts a powerful symbol of his African heritage appears to be more a case of Barlow's imposing his own politics on the song texts and then giving Johnson the credit. To the extent that Johnson resisted cultural norms, he did so not in his song texts but in his lifestyle, turning his back on farmwork and earning a living as a walking musician in an era of strict racial oppression and segregation. And for yet another thing, the devil, the symbol that Barlow identified as the "ultimate trickster figure in Johnson's blues," shows up in only one recorded song. As we will demonstrate later, Johnson's use of the devil in that song can be, and probably should be, interpreted in ways that are more in line with the American blues tradition.

In equating the African Legba (or Eshu) to the European Satan, Barlow probably felt he was on solid ground, because such cross-cultural equations were once fashionable in American anthropological and literary circles. But Gerhard Kubik, an ethnomusicologist and cultural anthropologist who has done extensive field research throughout sub-Saharan West Africa, says the devil in African American folklore is not a transplanted version of Legba or Eshu. Authors who attempt to show otherwise, says Kubik, are engaging in "freewheeling thought associations" that ignore the complexity of African cultures: "African-American studies seem often to pass through a stage in which the cognitive worlds of several distinctive African cultures are mixed up and grossly reinterpreted by the authors, with the Guinea Coast and particularly Nigeria providing the most easily accessible materials."[6]

Mary Ellison, in her 1989 book *Extensions of the Blues,* referred to the text of "Hellhound on My Trail" and then wrote: "Johnson was like no other singer. His imagery could be stark enough to be horrific and was made even more menacing by his use of the walking bass figure that was to become a common feature of Chicago blues."[7]

Where Ellison found Johnson's guitar figure to be menacing, however, Johnson's fellow musicians—pianist Sunnyland Slim for one—found his "walking the basses" to be an ingenious musical shorthand to help drive the beat, especially on up-tempo numbers. Muddy Waters, strongly influenced by Johnson's recordings, if not Johnson himself, remembered: "He had a different thing. Where we'd play it slow, Robert Johnson had it up tempo. The young idea of it, y'know what I mean."[8]

Johnny Shines and Robert "Junior" Lockwood said it seemed obvious to them that Johnson's guitar figures were adapted from the piano. According to Shines, "Anything a fellow could do on a piano, he could do it on the guitar."[9] Lockwood, the only musician known to have received instruction from Johnson, said: "Robert played the guitar like a piano— that was the difference. And other guitar players wasn't playing like that.

. . . Once I realized what he was doing, I've always known why he was special."[10]

Here again we are struck by the undeniable fact that musicians who knew Johnson and were steeped in the soundscape that informed Johnson's work heard his music differently than did the literary critics. The conflict between Johnson's latter-day interpreters and the musicians who heard and worked with him during his lifetime first became evident, as noted earlier, in Paul Oliver's *Conversations with the Blues*. The conflict continued, stubbornly unresolved, in most of the subsequent writing on Johnson, as writers unfamiliar with the blues tradition tried to relate Johnson's songs to what they learned in their college English courses. The exercise probably made Johnson's music more enjoyable, or at least more accessible, to the writers. But it also led them to interpret Johnson's lyrics in romanticized contexts that were never intended and to liken Johnson to an outlandish set of poets, philanderers, tragic heroes, and debauchers, including Orpheus, Shakespeare, John Donne, Arthur Rimbaud, Percy Bysshe Shelley, John Keats, Albert Camus, Jean-Paul Sartre, Gerard Manley Hopkins, Herman Melville, and inevitably, the Antichrist.

As the blues artist Julio Finn has pointed out, the Robert Johnson story hinges on the question of cultural reference points.[11] Latter-day fans are, of course, free to apply their own reference points and give whatever meanings they wish to Johnson's art; that kind of interaction between artist and audience always has been, and always will be, the dynamic wild card in any creative process. But we argue that the key to Johnson's music, especially for anyone who plans to write authoritatively about it, is not just the feeling it evokes in the solitary listener. One also needs to know something about the time and place in which Johnson performed and the mainly rural, mainly African American people with whom he commiserated over the wayward nature of men and women, the hardships of day-to-day life, and the fragility of relationships. For some reason most critics and interpreters have been reluctant to consider Johnson in such a context. From their perspective, whatever a Robert Johnson blues means to current listeners is just as valid as what it meant to Johnson and his audiences. But even if we accept the contemporary listener's experience as part of the creative equation, that still implies a mediation—

meeting an artist like Robert Johnson at least halfway. That's the trouble with romantics. Instead of meeting Johnson halfway, they seem determined to segregate him completely from his cultural roots, representing him as the singular artist, outside tradition, singing mainly of his own painful experiences and haunted thoughts. If such representations had any basis in fact, why was Johnson so respected by the traditional blues artists who heard him and worked with him? How was Johnson able to communicate so engagingly with the jook-joint audiences who came to hear him play?

Johnson's biographer Peter Guralnick, too, was struck by the contrast between the Johnson legend and the testimony of family members and others who knew Johnson. "For them the real Robert Johnson exists lodged firmly in memory," Guralnick observed. "For the rest of us he remains to be invented." [12]

In fact, the duality of the person and the invention, the former rooted in memory and the latter rooted in imagination, had been echoing through the literature since 1965. By the end of the eighties the invention—the image of Johnson as a darkly tormented man who wanted his contemporaries to believe that he had bartered away his soul—was moving inexorably to eclipse the person.

The Mississippi blues artist David "Honeyboy" Edwards, in a photo taken
during the Smithsonian Institution's 1991 Festival of American Folklife.
Edwards received a National Heritage Fellowship in 2002. (Smithsonian
photo)

Johnny Shines, one of Johnson's occasional traveling companions, performs at the 1991 Festival of American Folklife in Washington, D.C. Shines died in 1992. (Smithsonian photo)

The guitar and piano player Henry Townsend, another participant in the 1991 Smithsonian festival, worked with Johnson in St. Louis in the thirties. (NCTA photo, Kathy James)

Robert "Junior" Lockwood got to know Johnson during the time he was seeing Lockwood's mother and is the only artist known to have received guitar instruction from Johnson. (Smithsonian photo)

Big Joe Williams was the quintessential "walking musician." Born in Craw-
ford, Mississippi, in 1903, Williams was a road warrior for more than five
decades, working with artists as diverse as Peetie Wheatstraw, Robert Night-
hawk, Charlie Musselwhite, and Bob Dylan. (Smithsonian photo)

Although the Three Forks Store, twelve miles southwest of Greenwood near state Route 7, was once believed by some researchers to be the site of Robert Johnson's final gig, it's doubtful that Johnson ever played there. The building that once housed the store, converted to a residence once the store closed, was demolished within a year after this photo was taken in 2000. (McCulloch photo)

Not far from the site of the former Three Forks Store, a small flat gravestone, often adorned with guitar picks and coins left by passing blues pilgrims, marks the spot identified in 1990 as Robert Johnson's final resting place. The site, located next to Payne Chapel M. B. Church in the rural hamlet of Quito, was picked out by one of Johnson's long-ago girlfriends, whose testimony is no longer regarded as reliable. (McCulloch photo)

North of Morgan City, not far from the banks of the Yazoo River, Columbia Records installed this memorial in front of Mount Zion M. B. Church. The site was selected in 1991 on the basis of Johnson's death certificate, which said he was buried at "Zion Church." If Johnson died in the Greenwood vicinity, however, it is unlikely that his body would have been transported almost all the way to Morgan City for burial. (McCulloch photo)

ROBERT L. JOHNSON
MAY 8, 1911 ~ AUGUST 16, 1938
-musician & composer-
he influenced millions beyond his time

Jesus of Nazareth, King of Jerusalem,
I know that my Redeemer liveth and that
He will call me from the Grave.
...HANDWRITTEN BY ROBERT JOHNSON, SHORTLY BEFORE HIS DEATH AND PRESERVED
AMONG FAMILY PAPERS BY HIS SISTER, CARRIE H. THOMPSON

Commissioned by Johnson's biographer Stephen LaVere, this memorial now stands in the cemetery next to Little Zion M. B. Church just north of Greenwood. The cemetery is the most recently identified—and most likely—site of Johnson's burial in August 1938. The artist is thought to have died at a residence on Star of the West Plantation, which adjoined the church property. (McCulloch photo)

Jook houses, like this one in Shelby, are still common in the Mississippi Delta, but live music is probably less common than it was before World War II. In jook houses nowadays, patrons are more likely to be entertained by juke boxes. (McCulloch photo)

8   Reissue, Phase Three;
      or, Fifteen Minutes of Fame

> People making a lot of money all off these rumors.
> —Robert "Junior" Lockwood, quoted in *Can't You Hear the Wind Howl?*

The 1990 release of *Robert Johnson: The Complete Recordings* constituted a milestone along the Johnson paper trail. The liner notes for the boxed CD set included an 8,000-word biography written by Stephen LaVere, considered one of the primary researchers on Johnson's life. At last all the primary sleuths had at least some of their field research in print: LaVere in the liner notes; Stephen Calt and Gayle Dean Wardlow in *78 Quarterly;* Peter Guralnick in *Searching for Robert Johnson;* Jas Obrecht in the 1990 book *Blues Guitar: The Men Who Made the Music;* and Mack McCormick, indirectly, through the writings of Guralnick, Robert Palmer, and others. Even with McCormick's unpublished research material still at large, it appeared the quest was finally over. Three substantial biographies were available. The photographs had been found, bought, copyrighted, and published. And with yet another alternative take having been recovered, all Johnson's recorded songs were now at hand. Could this be the end of the mystery? Well, no.

Unexpectedly the *Complete Recordings* took off to become a runaway best seller, catching Sony Corporation, Columbia's new owner, off guard—but only briefly. The company quickly saw the market potential and resuscitated the Johnson legend. Larry Cohn, the producer of Columbia's Roots n' Blues series, noted: "You have an overwhelming mythology here. The whole selling-his-soul-to-the-devil routine seems very pervasive and sticks with people."[1]

And did it ever stick. In what amounted to a media feeding frenzy, critics and journalists of every stripe offered their own takes on the Robert Johnson story, turning 1990 into the year of the most hysterical Johnson hype yet. The hooks were irresistible: sex, booze, blues, Satan, rock and roll, scary music. There was something for almost everyone. Rockers found a challenging new guitar virtuoso to admire, armchair shrinks found a new subject to psychoanalyze, and even the religious right got into the act, finding new evidence of the link between Satan and rock and roll. Sadly, Robert Johnson, the man and blues musician who worked his art on street corners and in jooks across the South, was lost in the whirlwind of allegory and invention.

As 1990 drew to a close, *Living Blues* devoted an entire issue to Johnson's life and lore. The feature article, compiled by then editor Peter Lee and others, focused on Johnson's death. The essay included new "research," such as an interview with an older African American woman named Queen Elizabeth, identified by some sources as one of Johnson's long-ago girlfriends, who asserted that Johnson—and, it seemed, almost everybody else who sang blues—had gone straight to hell.[2] The Queen's testimony, though devout, was interesting mainly to folklorists and anthropologists, but the piece did show how desperately the compilers were willing to search for someone—anyone—to corroborate the dark side of the Johnson legend. Most telling of all were the compilers' allusions to Johnson as "the phantom bluesman" and Lee's reassurance to readers: "Our story on Johnson's death, while bringing you new information, does nothing to destroy the myths surrounding his life. But what would Johnson's blues be without the myth? Would we still be as mesmerized by his music—and the power and poetry of his blues—if there were no mystery surrounding his life?"[3]

Based on the great feeding frenzy of 1990 and the events that followed in 1991, the correct answer was no. By now the mythology had consumed reality and was feeding on itself. That Johnson had made a pact with the devil finally could be called "common knowledge," all of which helped to fuel the artist's brief fling as a popular-culture icon more than fifty years after his death. The *Complete Recordings* earned a Grammy Award as 1990's best historical album. Johnson was proclaimed "The Father of Rock and Roll" on the cover of *Musician* magazine in January 1991.[4] That same month, he earned a mention in *People* magazine's "Picks and Pans" feature, in which he was characterized as "equal parts hellhound and dreamer" with "the genius to make us feel his life in his songs."[5] Also in January, the *Complete Recordings* became a gold album, with sales in excess of a half-million CD sets—a figure that would rise to one million before the end of 1994.

Johnson's notoriety boosted public interest in blues. Samuel Charters seized the opportunity to put out a new book, *The Blues Makers,* which comprised two earlier books, *The Bluesmen,* first published in 1967, and *Sweet as Showers of Rain,* published in 1977. In an effort to bring things up to date, Charters added a new essay, "Robert Johnson: A New Consideration." In it he wrote, "Essentially there isn't any real mystery now about Robert Johnson." But then, in crediting Johnson for creating some of the "most haunting and magnificent moments" in blues, Charters concluded: "It is these moments which will always be the mystery."[6]

Charters tried, but he just couldn't bring himself to drop the mystery angle entirely. Nor could he resist closing on a flight of reverie: "Perhaps the best way to remember him is to think of him getting out of bed in the middle of the night to pick up his guitar. Sometimes the girl he was staying with would wake up and see him sitting by the window, silently fingering the guitar in the moonlight. If he turned around and saw she was watching him he would stop."[7] The only real difference between this and Rudi Blesh's lurid rhapsody in 1946 is that our hero has at last been allowed to come indoors. And he has company.

The Search for Robert Johnson, produced for British commercial television in 1992, extended the Johnson paper trail into the area of "documentary style" film. John Hammond, the musician son of the man who once tried to book Johnson for a Carnegie Hall concert, narrated the film and also appeared on screen, playing the role of a blues musician who travels through the Mississippi Delta looking for scraps of information about Johnson—a screenplay based loosely on the field research of Mack McCormick. Hammond hooked up with Johnny Shines, David "Honeyboy" Edwards, and other Johnson contemporaries, questioning them to discover what kind of man Johnson was, what kind of musician he was, how he traveled, and how he died. Hammond also got to sing a few of Johnson's songs.

The film was an important addition to the paper trail, but for a reason that had nothing to do with Hammond's onscreen interpretations of Johnson's music: It was the first document to contain unfiltered testimony from McCormick, an important Johnson researcher whose work had never before been published under his own name. Along with Gayle Dean Wardlow, McCormick appeared in the film as an authoritative talking head, popping in from time to time to offer insights about Johnson and the culture in which he lived. Offering what was easily the most startling piece of new information in the film, McCormick reported that the satanic legends about Johnson, far from being tall tales concocted by other people, were stories with which the artist consciously chose to associate himself because, as McCormick phrased it, he was "drawn to that texture of 'I am with the devil—me and the devil walking side by side.'" It all started, according to McCormick, with the death of Johnson's first wife, Virginia. When she died in childbirth, Johnson was not at her side but off somewhere trying to earn money as a musician. For this, McCormick asserted, Johnson was held up to "incredible community condemnation" among Virginia's friends and family members because they felt he was an "evil musician" whose pursuit of a godless lifestyle had contributed to his wife's death. Johnson, confronted with this dark image of himself, eventually made a calculated decision to "associate himself with the things that had been condemned." Here is where the quasi-documentary format of the film became troublesome. McCormick's take on the Johnson legend was served up as revealed truth, with no attribution, no explanation, and no opportunity to assess the credibility of sources. And in the years since the film was first aired on British television, no other researcher has unearthed material to corroborate McCormick's version.

One assumes that McCormick's source material will be fully explicated when his book, *Biography of a Phantom*, is published, but until then we can only wonder about the source of this unique account of Johnson's life. In the TV film two former Johnson girlfriends were called on to provide testimony concerning the satanic pact. Willie Mae Powell[8] said her cousin, the bluesman Honeyboy Edwards, once told her "it's the truth" that Johnson "sold himself in the forks of the road, twelve o'clock at night. . . . He did it. He wanted to be a sworn musician, and that scound' could play anything." She concluded with a wistful laugh. In addition, the aforementioned Queen Elizabeth (see chapter 7) said she once asked Johnson straight out about the crossroads, and he supposedly replied, "That's where you have to play." Queen Elizabeth, not laughing wistfully or otherwise, concluded with one of her heartfelt sermons on the perdition that awaits all musicians, including the interviewer Hammond, who sing blues. All this was served up with atmospheric background supplied by Hammond, standing in the middle of a rural crossroads, playing a National steel-body guitar, and singing "Cross Road Blues."

Without impugning Willie Mae Powell's recollection, it can be noted that in another section of the film, she described how pleasant Johnson was, giving the impression that if she knew about a devil deal at the time, or if Johnson was actively encouraging the notion that he had bartered his soul to Satan, it failed to dampen her affection for the artist. It is possible she did not know about any crossroads bargain until Edwards told her many years after Johnson's death, when both she and Edwards were targeted as valuable sources of information on Johnson's life and when the Faustian angle was emerging as a powerful marketing tool for Johnson's music.

As for the consistency of Honeyboy Edwards's accounts, he made no mention of a crossroads deal in a 1968 interview with Pete Welding, in an interview published in *Living Blues* in 1970–71, or in an interview with Pearson in 1979. Perhaps Edwards didn't say anything because he wasn't asked, although he was presented with a golden opportunity in the 1968 interview when Welding asked, "Did he [Johnson] ever tell you how he learned to play?" Edwards replied, "Yeah, he would talk about it," and then segued into unrelated recollections.[9] It is surprising that Welding did not press the issue since, at that time, he was the only writer who had published a direct suggestion of a supernatural bargain in Johnson's musical evolution. Much more surprising is the fact that Edwards offered no comment about a crossroads deal in the British documentary film, even though he spent considerable time on camera and supplied information about other aspects of Johnson's life and death.[10] Edwards must have been asked. If he wasn't, it was a lamentable oversight given the fact that his cousin Willie Mae Powell had cited him as the source for her story.

John Hammond, notwithstanding his willingness to appear in dramatic crossroads and graveyard scenes in the film, was already on record as a disbeliever. In an earlier interview with the writer Tony Scherman, Hammond said all his conversations with musicians who had known Johnson led him to conclude that Johnson had been an upbeat, positive person (except when he was drinking) and that stories about a satanic pact were "all crap."[11]

In the British film McCormick also added a dramatic new element to the Johnson death stories, revealing that he had found Johnson's killer. McCormick said he had been questioning someone about Johnson's death when the man he was interviewing suddenly provided an elaborate account of his whereabouts on the night Johnson was poisoned. McCormick said he pointed out that the story was a patently obvious alibi, at which point the man broke down and confessed. Just like that. McCormick declined to identify the suspect: "No, can't do that—I don't want to get into a legal situation that that would bring about."

Although most of the details of Johnson's death had come to light by 1993 (except, of course, for the identity of McCormick's suspect), that year brought a new account of the artist's final moments, an account so unusual in so many different ways that it warrants close examination. The account, published by the famed folklorist Alan Lomax in his book *The Land Where the Blues Began,* started in Memphis, where Lomax said he stopped in 1942 on his way to document traditional music in Coahoma County, Mississippi. While in Memphis Lomax reportedly ran across a William Brown whom he believed to be Johnson's "friend boy Willie Brown"

mentioned in a recording of "Cross Road Blues." By Lomax's account, Brown had not yet heard that Johnson was dead, which seems improbable but certainly not impossible. In any case, Brown supposedly put Lomax on the trail of Robert Johnson's mother. Lomax said he went to meet the woman at her home near Tunica, Mississippi. According to Lomax, she recalled her dismay over "Little Robert's" attraction to secular music, said she had always known he would come to no good end, and recounted how, finally, she was called to the place where he lay dying: "When I went in where he at, he layin up in bed with his guitar crost his breast. Soon's he saw me, he say, 'Mama, you all I been waitin for. Here,' he say, and he give me his guitar, 'take and hang this thing on the wall, cause I done pass all that by. That what got me messed up, mama. It's the devil's instrument, just like you said. And I don't want it no more.' And he died while I was hangin it on the wall."

Even though Lomax told fellow folklorists that he had found Johnson's mother, his only full account of the meeting was the one in *The Land Where the Blues Began,* published fifty-one years after the fact. The account, which reads like a screenplay and includes a five-hundred-word direct quote, is reminiscent of John H. Hammond Jr.'s dramatic 1938 deathbed scene (with Vocalion record representatives breaking the news of the Carnegie Hall booking just as Johnson breathed his final breath) in that it arouses immediate skepticism. Did this tale originate with Lomax or the woman he interviewed? How did Lomax remember dialogue so well after fifty years? Or was the conversation recorded and transcribed? And if it was, where is the raw transcription?

Most other accounts depict Johnson's mother as being told of her son's death after the fact, not standing at bedside awaiting his dying words. But Lomax's account certainly makes for a better story, since it brings redemptive closure to a sinner's life. Lomax concluded his half-century-old reminiscence thus: "Her slim brown feet, the last vestige of her beauty, raised little puffs of dust as she danced about the yard, calling on the Lord and Little Robert. She had forgotten me. She was happy. She was shouting, possessed and in ecstasy. And so I left her."[12]

Lomax's treatment is problematic for historical purposes, not least because he identified the woman he interviewed as "Mary Johnson."[13] Was this a stepmother? Was she another wife of one of Johnson's stepfathers,

or possibly a wife of Johnson's real father? Did she even know our Robert, or was she the mother of another Robert Johnson? Or is it possible
that Lomax simply waited too long to reconstruct the interview and placed
too much trust in his own memory? Did Lomax get the name from the
woman herself or from some other source? (In a field note written at the
time, Lomax identified her only as "Robert Johnson's mother.") In the
absence of definitive answers to such questions, there is at least one observation that should be noted: Discrepancies exist between the field research Lomax purported to chronicle in *The Land Where the Blues Began*
and his own field notes and other documentation related to the research.

In a field note, for example, Lomax wrote: "We went with him [blues-
man Son House] to see Robert Johnson's mother. She told us of her son,
spoke of God her great master, got happy as we left prophesying in the
dusty yard." In the 1993 book, however, Lomax indicates that he was alone
when he went to visit "Mary Johnson." House doesn't show up until the
next section of the book, in which Lomax tells of recording House at a
country store near Tunica, Mississippi. Lomax says House was joined at
the session by a string band that included, "to [his] surprise, William
Brown"—the same William Brown that Lomax says he first encountered
in Memphis in June 1942 on his way to Coahoma County. But song transcriptions and other session documentation show that the country-store
session with House took place in August 1941 near Lake Cormorant, the
year before Lomax says he traced the whereabouts of Johnson's mother.
So Lomax should not have been surprised to meet William Brown at the
store because he had not yet encountered Brown near Memphis. Rather,
he should have been surprised to see Brown in Memphis, because by
then he would have known Brown from the store session. After the 1941
store session, at which Lomax was assisted by his wife, Elizabeth, Lomax
did record House again in 1942. Perhaps for narrative purposes, Lomax
moved the store scene from Lake Cormorant to Tunica.

Even putting aside such discrepancies, one troubling point remains:
Assuming Lomax believed in 1942 that the woman he met was Johnson's
mother, and also assuming he got the name Mary Johnson from a good
source, maybe even the woman herself, he should have suspected by
1993 that something was fishy (or that his readers would need a more
detailed explanation), since by that time correct information about John-

son's mother, Julia Major Dodds, had been available for almost eleven years.

In the same book Lomax related how he happened to uncover a possible connection between Johnson and the Texas bluesman Blind Lemon Jefferson. (Lomax believed Jefferson to be a seminal figure in the evolution of the blues, so establishing such a connection would have lent support to a theory, then held by a few researchers and record collectors, that blues evolved along a line that started in Texas and moved to Mississippi.) Lomax said he interviewed Johnson's early mentor Son House, and House supposedly volunteered the information that he had taught Jefferson's songs and styles to Johnson after learning them from an older Clarksdale, Mississippi, musician called "Lemon" because of his ability to imitate Blind Lemon's recordings. (Research suggests that House did learn some of his slide techniques from a Clarksdale guitarist named Willie Wilson, but whether he also learned any of Jefferson's styles from Wilson is difficult to discern in House's recorded output.) The information supplied to Lomax by House raises familiar questions. Was the information diligently transcribed from a recording, or was this yet another of the "encounters and conversations . . . dimly recollected after fifty years," to which Lomax alluded in his preface? The author himself may have supplied a partial answer. In an early footnote he conceded that some readers might question the storylike form of the book but said that he had decided a "narrative account" would be the most effective way to present his scholarly conclusions concerning the emergence of blues and other regional styles.

Although Robert Johnson's posthumous flirtation with celebrity cooled after 1991, the artist never quite returned to his former place at the margin of popular music history. He was now America's best-known downhome, prewar Delta blues musician. The transition from obscurity to acknowledged old master, far from sparking interest in the real facts about Johnson's life, only guaranteed the persistence of the legend.

9   A Myth to the Twenty-first Century

"My name's Johnson," the black man said. "Robert Johnson."
"It's good to meet you, Mr. Johnson. Who's your traveling
partner?"
Johnson picked up his guitar, held it close to his body.
"My best friend," Johnson said. "But I ain't gonna tell y'all
his name. The Gentleman might hear and come runnin'. He
gets into the strings, you hear?"

—Sherman Alexie, *Reservation Blues*

By the start of the new millennium, the Johnson legend had
shown up in two novels, three documentary films, advertis-
ing, journalism, and popular music. It had also shown up in
two screenplays: *Crossroads,* the Ralph Macchio vehicle that
was produced as a movie in 1986; and *Love in Vain: A Vision of Robert Johnson,* which, at this writing, remains an un-
produced script. Written by Alan Greenberg and originally
published in the early eighties, *Love in Vain* was reprinted
in 1994 with a new foreword by movie director Martin Scorsese, who likened Greenberg's version of Johnson to a "haunted prophet who must go into the desert to find his voice,
and who plays his music not out of choice but because he
has no choice; he has become possessed by the spirit of the
blues."[1] While following the general contours of Johnson's
biography in the context of the Great Depression, Greenberg's script offered a surrealistic compilation of blues he-

roes, song and sermon fragments, and African American folk beliefs cast against an alternately forbidding and comic backdrop in which the dead speak and musicians strum stringless guitars. The screenplay, like Sherman Alexie's 1995 novel *Reservation Blues,* treated Johnson's life in terms of myth and ritual and read like a morality play—or perhaps a morality musical.

Reservation Blues was obviously a work of fiction. *Love in Vain* was labeled a "vision." These two works stood apart from the less-clearly-labeled visions that had gained legitimacy in scholarly discourse and documentary film. Labeling hardly mattered by that time, though, because the crossroads legend had metastasized into popular culture, becoming so widely known and so casually accepted that it no longer required attribution, skepticism, or scholarly trappings.

In 1995 *The New Rolling Stone Encyclopedia of Rock and Roll* confidently asserted in its entry on Johnson: "He often claimed he learned to play guitar from the Devil himself and many of his recordings evince a haunting, otherworldly inspiration."[2] Soon afterward Sandra B. Tooze, in her 1997 book on Muddy Waters, first alluded to Johnson's unholy trade with a prudent disclaimer: "Then, as the legend goes, Johnson made a date with the devil." In her truncated summary of Johnson's life and death, however, Tooze let romantic imagery take precedence over objectivity: "Johnson fought off the devil's final grip for several days, until Satan claimed his own on 16 August, 1938. He died with his guitar across his heart."[3] (We are struck by this last touching detail. The only similar account of Johnson's death is the rather dubious one found in Alan Lomax's *Land Where the Blues Began,* but recall that in his version Johnson's mother removed the guitar from her son's chest and hung it on the wall just as the artist expired.)

As we near the end of our journey along the Johnson paper trail and prepare to take a fresh look at Johnson's music and life, here are some examples of the way the artist is most often portrayed in contemporary writing. It would be possible, we suspect, to fill several pages with this sort of thing, but five brief examples will drive the point home.

In 1999 the musicologist Gerhard Kubik joked about how difficult it had been to finish his book *Africa and the Blues:* "Robert Johnson appeared to me . . . and proposed a simple solution to my problem: I had better sign up with the devil and I would finish the work successfully."[4] Also in 1999, the cultural critic and hip-hop guru Nelson George mentioned "Robert Johnson selling his soul to the devil at midnight in Mississippi" in the context of writing about heroes and antiheroes in his 1999 book *Hip Hop America.*[5]

How about a sports reference? In late 1999 *Tennis* magazine ran an article suggesting a possible parallel between Robert Johnson and the four-time U.S. Open champion John McEnroe—"each selling his soul to the devil in order to make violently graceful black magic with his instrument."[6]

In June 2000, when the Mississippi Supreme Court ruled that Claud Johnson (the child born to Vergie Mae Smith on December 12, 1931) was Robert Johnson's son and sole legal heir, reporter Rick Bragg's story for the New York Times News Service didn't even mention the news hook until the fifth paragraph. What did Bragg emphasize instead? Here's the lead paragraph: "JACKSON, Miss.—The legend was that if you touched Robert Johnson you could feel the talent running through him, like heat, put there by the devil on a dark delta crossroad in exchange for his soul. It is why Claud Johnson's grandparents would not let him out of the house that day in 1937 when Robert Johnson, his father, strolled into the yard."[7]

As a crowning touch, a wire editor at the *Washington Post* headlined Bragg's story this way: "Court Rules Father of the Blues Has Son." After being invented and reinvented as naïve genius, folk singer, the last of the country bluesmen, nut cake, and the inventor of rock and roll, Robert Johnson finally usurped the title "father of the blues," an honorific previously reserved for the composer W. C. Handy (who conferred it on himself) and Mississippi blues artist Charley Patton.

And in July 2001, in a newspaper feature about the absence of Delta-style blues in the one-time cradle of the blues around Clarksdale, Mississippi, a Canadian writer identified Johnson as "the mythical figure who sold his soul to the devil at the crossroads just outside of Clarksdale."[8]

As these recent references illustrate, the romantic notions ultimately triumphed over the less captivating facts about the way Johnson acquired his musical talent, and the crossroads legend became a piece of Americana.

10 Satan and Sorcery

I want to take a journey to the devil down below.
—Bessie Smith (1927)

Twenty-nine songs, recorded in 1936 and 1937, provide the
body of evidence most often cited to support the themes
of supernatural torment and Faustian tragedy in Johnson's
life.

Yet a review of all the critical writing since the midfor-
ties shows a strange preoccupation with just two of the
twenty-nine songs. One of the two, "Me and the Devil Blues,"
stands alone as the only Johnson song to contain specific
references to Satan and the devil. The other song, "Hellhound on My Trail," contains references to being driven and
on the move, but those references are open to various interpretations, not all of them dark or terrifying, as we will
show shortly when we examine Johnson's recorded songs.
Is it really fair to portray Johnson as an artist who believed
in sorcery and the supernatural, possibly including a belief
that he was locked in a relationship with Satan, on the basis
of one or two song texts?

Viewing Johnson's songs in historical perspective, it is
worth noting that devil references in blues were common
in the late thirties and early forties; you might even say

there was a minicraze of devil songs. When Johnson worked in St. Louis in 1935, he had opportunities to hear Lonnie Johnson, Peetie Wheatstraw, and Charlie Jordan, three artists who recorded songs containing references to hell and the devil. Lonnie Johnson, whose stylings were clearly emulated by Robert, recorded at least three: "She's Making Whoopee in Hell Tonight" (1930), "Hell Is a Name for All Sinners" (1931), and "Devil's Got the Blues" (1938). Wheatstraw recorded "Devil's Son in Law" (1931), "Devilment Blues" (1937), and "Peetie Wheatstraw Stomp" (1937), in which he declared himself the "high sheriff of hell." Charlie Jordan had "Hell-bound Blues" (1932). Tampa Red, based in Chicago, recorded three such tunes between 1934 and 1941, and John Lee "Sonny Boy" Williamson recorded at least two. The list goes on.

In most of these songs the devil was not a source of terror but a convenient shared reference, often offered in a humorous context, to explain or characterize a woman's actions. One could argue that Robert Johnson's devil references were more serious, or more visual, or that his references loom larger in music history because we believe in him or because he achieved legend status while many of his contemporaries did not. But for the sake of comparison, consider another legend, the blues diva Bessie Smith. She died one year earlier than Johnson and is the only other blues artist who commands a comparable mythology. Like Johnson, Smith embodied virtually every stereotype of the blues singer. And when Smith sang about hell or the devil, she left little to the imagination. In "Blue Spirit Blues" she sang, "The devil came and grabbed my hand . . . took me down to that red hot land," and also referred to demons with eyelids dripping blood. In "Send Me to the Electric Chair Blues" she sang, "I want to take a journey to the devil down below." In "Dying by the Hour" she sang of making a phone call to the devil. In "Black Mountain Blues" she boasted, "Got the devil in my soul and I'm full of bad booze." In "Devil Gonna Get You" she warned, "Mister devil's down below, pitchfork in his hand," and she sang about Satan in "Satan's Waiting for You All."

All told, Bessie Smith sang about Old Nick at least six times compared to Johnson's one—two if you insist on counting a non-sequitur subtitle, "Up Jumped the Devil," on his recording of "Preaching Blues." Smith's references were more direct than Johnson's. Yet it is Johnson, not Smith, who is mythologized by romantic critics as an artist who went to the crossroads and negotiated an unholy bargain with the devil. Once again, we see that Johnson is a special case.

Just to underscore that last point, note that Peetie Wheatstraw, a powerful bluesman whose real name was William Bunch, actively promoted the idea that he was in a relationship with Satan,[1] yet he and his songs are all but ignored by the romantics who flyspeck Robert Johnson's lyrics in search of evidence linking Johnson to the supernatural.

Romantics aren't the only ones who hear references to sorcery and the supernatural in Johnson's blues. Some scholars do as well. David Evans, for one, has devoted his life to studying the music and folklore of the Deep South. He finds explicit supernatural references in eight of Johnson's twenty-nine recorded songs—two more than Samuel Charters. And Evans believes similar references are "probably implied" in most of Johnson's other songs—"a far higher percentage," Evans asserts, "than in the work of any other blues composer."[2] Indeed, if Johnson's lyrics truly did mirror his life, says Evans, then "he lived in a world of fear, suspicion, and nightmares."[3]

But these conclusions appear to be largely a function of what Evans, with his superior knowledge of ethnic culture, is willing to accept as a probable reference. Take the subject of hoodoo. Evans stalks any possible link to hoodoo—overt, covert, or unintended. In the process, he creates a sense of solving a puzzle so difficult that only a master ethnodetective could spot the clues. Reviewing songs from Johnson's first recording session in 1936, Evans claims to find many references to sorcery but says they are so "allusive" that many listeners would probably be unaware of the underlying theme. Evans even includes Johnson's ethnic audiences in this group: "These consumers of his music were evidently not troubled by *or did not recognize* his cryptic references to sorcery" (emphasis added).[4]

Here is an example of the references Evans is willing to accept: He writes that any implied mention of impotence is suggestive of hoodoo because in folk belief hoodoo can cause impotence. By extension, one could just as easily argue that since hoodoo can cause lovers to separate, get back together, or think suspicious thoughts about each other, hoodoo is an active agent in practically every blues song ever composed, not just Johnson's.

The impotence-hoodoo connection weakens as a hallmark of Johnson's songwriting when one reviews the countless double-entendre blues in which someone's so-and-so won't such-and-such no more. It is clear from these and other references that hoodoo not only permeates blues humor but is also a common motif throughout the tradition—all of which seems to render Johnson's lyrics more in the mainstream than at the extreme.

Another example: In "Kindhearted Woman Blues," the first song Johnson ever cut, Evans targets the phrase "she studies evil all the time" as suggestive of "secret plotting and sorcery."[5] But another researcher, Stephen Calt, reads *evil* here as a once-common African American colloquialism for "spitefulness." In most traditional blues usage, the word, when applied to a woman, relates more to contrariness or unwillingness to comply and can usually be read in a lighter, less malevolent vein. As for the verb *studies,* it is also a common blues usage and is synonymous with "thinks about," Calt says.[6] "I ain't studying about you" would be a typical example.

Johnson's "I Believe I'll Dust My Broom," the second song he recorded in 1936, receives similar treatment from Evans, deconstructed outside general blues language. Evans says the phrase "dust my broom . . . could suggest an actual magic practice of riddance."[7] To be sure, the broom is connected with many folk beliefs and superstitions, but the blues musician Big Joe Williams, who knew Johnson and was a devout believer in magic, said the phase meant simply "leaving for good . . . I'm putting you down, I won't be back no more."[8] Evans, too, notes that this is one possible interpretation of the phrase "dust my broom."

In "Come on in My Kitchen," the song that supposedly once brought a St. Louis audience to tears, Johnson mentioned taking his woman's last nickel from her "nation sack." Calt's research determined that the term came from "donation sack."[9] Evans traces the term back to a cloth or leather bag worn by Native American women. The bag, containing occult charms and other valuables, was worn close to a woman's pubic area, "reinforcing its magical symbolism," according to Evans.[10] Whether it's a donation sack or a Native American sack, a purse is still a purse. What Johnson sang was that his woman wouldn't be back because he took all her money from her purse.

For the sake of comparison—and also to make a point—let's consider the work of another blues composer, Willie Dixon, the vaunted "Black

Knight" of Chess Records. Dixon's songs contained numerous references to hoodoo and superstition, yet Dixon's songs, most of which were written for other Chess artists, have never been put under a microscope the way Johnson's have. That's because Dixon is generally thought to have been more artisan than artist—a clever writer, but sadly lacking in gravitas.

To put it another way, Dixon is regarded as a professional lyricist who made a conscious decision to write songs about mojos and brooms and other African American folk beliefs. Johnson, on the other hand, is regarded as a natural man, caught up in some sort of supernatural vortex, who had no choice but to sing songs about sorcery and evil and the demons that dogged his every footstep. When viewed through this haze of romanticism, Johnson's song texts become more pure, more authentic, because Johnson the artist was capable of singing only one thing: the Truth.

Okay, then, let's take a closer look at the recorded songs.

11   The Song Texts

[I] get home and get blue and start howling, and the hellhound get on my trail.

—J. T. "Funny Papa" Smith (1931)

As can be seen in the paper trail we have been following, most previous attempts to analyze Johnson's songs, either as works of art or as clues to the artist's inner life, have been flawed by the application of what one might call the Lord Byron model. Researchers and critics alike listen to Johnson's songs and profess to hear evidence of deep-seated anguish. Based on this anguish, Johnson is cast in the role of the doomed troubadour, a gifted but tormented loner whose very isolation made it possible for him to realize his own genius and achieve a profoundly personal artistic vision.

As noted by the historian and ethnic studies professor George Lipsitz, all such analyses hit wide of the mark: "Romanticist critics might prefer to imagine blues musicians as folk artists outside the culture industry, but in order to survive, much less record, they had to master the codes of commercial culture, even at the local level."[1]

Or especially at the local level.

Johnson was very much a folk artist, but he was also canny and business-like in his mastery of the codes of commercial culture, albeit largely within his own culture. If this seems inconsistent, try thinking of Johnson not as a folk artist but as an innovative "vernacular artist." He forged his art by drawing from African American tradition; from records, radio, and the other artists he met on his travels; and from his own creative imagination.

In our own examination of Johnson's song texts, then, we will emphasize the vernacular at the expense of the romantic. And we will place the songs in contexts that may help clarify how, or even whether, Johnson was influenced by his musical contemporaries, by his rural African American culture and its folk beliefs, by the exigencies of his itinerant lifestyle, and by the people who recorded him.

In all this we do well to remember that the defining event of Johnson's time was the Great Depression. The resulting misery, particularly in the rural South, undoubtedly confirmed Johnson's natural distaste for the peonage of sharecropping and helped stoke his interest in music as an alternative lifestyle. Even so, it is difficult today to imagine the resourcefulness, the sheer moxie, that allowed Johnson and other African American blues artists to survive as walking musicians in an era of racial oppression and unprecedented economic hardship.

Johnson's twenty-nine recorded songs derived from many sources, ranging from old work songs to the most up-to-date blues hits of his day. He played in an impressive variety of styles and, to the practiced ear, sang in several styles, probably depending on whom he was trying to emulate. His voice was lighter in texture than other artists from his region, such as Charlie Patton, Son House, Muddy Waters, or Elmore James, but he sang hard and with feeling. There was also a sexual quality to his tone and phrasing, and most of his songs were about women, if not directed toward them, balancing aggressive sexuality with pleas for understanding or sexual favors. As with most blues, a number of his songs were about leaving, traveling, or moving on.

Although Johnson is regarded as a Delta bluesman, he was actually a musical sponge with a gift for absorbing songs—lyrics as well as instrumental riffs—from other artists. Johnny Shines claimed Johnson could add a song to his repertoire after hearing it only once, an important skill considering the range of requests Johnson was likely to get when playing for a crowd on a street corner. But Johnson did more than just cover the material of other artists; he was remarkably adept at drawing what suited him from an array of sources and then melding the fragments into a personal statement through his own voice, his instrumental innovations, and his ability to project feeling. This ability, according to Shines, was showcased on Johnson's recordings:

> Some of the songs, I imagine, they wasn't all Robert Johnson's. Now there was a lot of guys around then was playing, you know. And he was doing some of everything you heard. If you liked it, you did it. So, no doubt, you go in the studio to record it. He just do the stuff that come to his mind, for instance, because he had no set plan for no recording session. He just record whatsoever come to his mind when he plays.
>
> Here's the thing about it, for instance, along in those times, maybe you stayed over here in this county. You played your kind of blues. . . . Way over in the next county I'm playing it another way. And maybe two or three guys in the same county was playing it different. . . . So a lots of numbers was done before. And everybody did their version.[2]

Asked about Johnson's repertoire, contemporaries remembered hearing him play many of the blues he later recorded. They also remembered ballads such as "Casey Jones" and "President McKinley," preblues dance numbers such as "Make Me a Pallet on the Floor," early blues such as "East St. Louis Blues" and "You Can Mistreat Me Here But You Can't When I Go Home," and more obscure songs such as "Captain George Did Your Money Come?" and "Black Gal, Whyn't You Comb Your Head?"[3] In addition, Shines and Robert "Junior" Lockwood recalled an extensive catalog of pop songs and country tunes, as well as blues, traditional and otherwise, that never made it onto his records.

Considering this expansive repertoire, there must have been plenty of songs from which to choose when Johnson showed up for his first recording session in San Antonio on November 23, 1936. Before looking at the output of that session, though, we ought to acknowledge the presence of Don Law, the British A&R supervisor who presided over all five of Johnson's sessions in 1936 and 1937. Whatever Law thought of Johnson, it would be naïve to overlook his input. As Arhoolie Records' producer Chris Strachwitz reminds us, "The A&R man's job is to help select and shape the songs the recording artist actually makes."[4] Law and the engineers shared a responsibility to see that the sessions flowed both artistically and technically. Law collaborated with the artist to select the numbers that would make the best records with the strongest sales potential while pushing to record as many songs as possible per session (Law and his crew recorded over one hundred sides during the first three days of the San Antonio setup).[5]

We have no way of knowing how receptive Johnson was to Law's input. But it is logical to assume that Law offered suggestions from time to time, just to keep the ball rolling. And it is probably fair to say that Law sometimes weighed in with suggestions after hearing the first take of a Johnson song, offering ideas that he thought would make subsequent takes better or at least more appealing to Vocalion's market in the Deep South. Steve LaVere discovered a test groove that picked up a fragment of conversation prior to take 1 of "Love in Vain." According to LaVere, Johnson said to Law, "I want to go on with our next one myself." Out of context the comment is difficult to interpret because it seems to contrast the collaborative *our* with the less collaborative *myself*. However read, the snippet implies interaction, or at least conversation, and possibly cooperation—and Johnson, our allegedly naïve country bumpkin, sounds rather secure.[6]

It is generally believed, though not confirmed, that first takes came closest to the way a blues artist performed pieces for his street-corner or jook-house audiences. Changes made in following takes were likely the result of collaboration between the artist and the A&R specialist. However many takes were tried, it was common practice to keep only the two that were deemed to be the best.

Of the five Johnson recording sessions, the first most plainly belonged to the artist. Law's input, if any, was minimal. Johnson showed up with a clear idea of what he wanted to record, and the resulting session yielded his finest material, his most representative work, and four songs that would become traditional standards: "Kindhearted Woman Blues," "I Believe I'll Dust My Broom," "Sweet Home Chicago," and "Ramblin' on My Mind." Also recorded at the session were "When You Got a Good Friend," "Come On in My Kitchen," "Terraplane Blues" (his biggest-selling race record), and "Phonograph Blues."

Examining the texts, we see that the songs from that session deal with mistreatment, leaving, travel, seduction, and sex but contain no references to anything overtly supernatural or violent. In one of the takes of "Ramblin' on My Mind" Johnson refers to "devilment"[7] on his baby's mind, as well as "mean things" on his own mind. But in the song Johnson opts for leaving, and the mean things, whatever they are, never get enacted.

One scholar, David Evans, sees a veiled reference to sorcery in Johnson's use of the word *trick* in "Sweet Home Chicago": "You going keep on monkeying around here, friend boy, you going get your business all in a trick" and, in the next verse, "Friend boy, she trick you one time she sure going do it again."[8] Given the many nonsupernatural meanings of *trick* in both American and African American slang, plus the contexts in which the word appears in "Sweet Home Chicago," Johnson probably was not warning about the power of evil spirits; he was more likely telling his "friend boy" that he could either come along to "the land of California" or stay put and continue to be duped and deceived. An even more mundane explanation for one of the references to *trick* is that Johnson simply incorporated a rhyme—*six* and *trick(ed)*—that he picked up from Kokomo Arnold's 1934 recording of "Old Original Kokomo Blues," the song on which "Sweet Home Chicago" is based.

After an absence of two days, during which Johnson may have been cooling his heels in jail after a run-in with San Antonio police, the artist returned to the recording studio for his second and third sessions. Those sessions, November 26 and 27, 1936, yielded "32–20 Blues," "They're Red Hot," "Dead Shrimp Blues," "Cross Road Blues," "Walkin' Blues," "Last Fair Deal Gone Down," "Preaching Blues," and "If I Had Possession over Judgment Day." The dominant topics, once again, were mistreatment, travel, sex, and betrayal, but at least four of these songs were later cited as evi-

dence of the violent or supernatural forces that somehow shaped Johnson's personality. Let's examine the evidence:

1. "32–20 Blues": This is a reworking of "22–20 Blues," recorded by Skip
James. True enough, the song text presents a sequence of threatened violence and asks whether Johnson or his woman has the bigger gun. But
in this battle of the sexes, no shots are fired—no one wins and no one
loses.

2. "If I Had Possession over Judgment Day": Paul Oliver claimed to
hear evidence of Johnson's "tormented spirit" here,[9] but the melody is
straight out of the blues tradition and is known to most folks as "Rolling
and Tumbling," the Delta national anthem. The verses focus on mistreatment and seduction. Johnson suggests, perhaps irreverently, that if he had
the power, he would render a harsh verdict on his fickle girlfriend, "who
wouldn't have no right to pray." But there is no hint of Faustian angst.

3. "Preaching Blues": This is a reworking of Son House's similarly titled
song. In Johnson's version the blues is personified—it walks in "like a man"
in the morning and causes all sorts of heartache. It is a powerful blues,
loaded with instrumental pyrotechnics, and Johnson sings it in a raspy, impassioned vocal style, perhaps emulating his former mentor House. But
the themes of the song are traditional and secular, making it difficult to
comprehend why the song was parenthetically subtitled "Up Jumped the
Devil," the name of a Texas fiddle tune recorded in San Antonio by the
Tune Wranglers a month before Johnson's sessions.[10] Western swing groups
were being recorded around the same time as Johnson was, so maybe it
was an erroneous transposition of titles. Or perhaps the energized tempo
of "Preaching Blues" suggested the need for an alternative dance title. Or
maybe someone wanted to distance the piece from House's version, issued six years earlier on Paramount. It doesn't really matter; except for the
inexplicable subtitle, the song makes no reference to anything supernatural or, in contrast to the House version, anticlerical. Yet the song has been
implicated by the legend makers anyway on grounds that Johnson's singing is incoherent, a possible sign of possession and dark, hidden mystery.

4. "Cross Road Blues": Of all the songs recorded at the San Antonio
sessions, this one has proven to be the most heavily laden with satanic
symbolism, at least to critics, folk-revival fans, and some of today's rock-
influenced fans. Stephen Calt suggests Johnson may have been doing the

song as early as 1932. If so, it was a mainstay in his repertoire. It makes no mention of anything diabolical but garners its dark reputation—which is then projected back onto the singer—from European and African folk beliefs about the supernatural qualities of crossroads. In neo-African lore the crossroads is the realm of Legba, who serves as gatekeeper or mediator between the secular sphere and the spirit domain. According to African American folklore, one can go to a crossroads (usually *the* crossroads) and make a deal with the devil or some other supernatural entity: your soul in exchange for musical talent, for example. These unholy bargains also can be struck in graveyards, deep in the woods, or even under certain trees—typically oak, dogwood, or holly—and the ritual may have to be enacted more than once to be effective. In Johnson's case, both the crossroads and the graveyard have been suggested as ritual sites. But in none of his recorded blues did the artist ever sing, "I went down to the graveyard" (even though it's a common blues line). He did sing, "I went down to the crossroads," so that is the site that has been anointed in the official canon of legends as the place where Johnson bartered his soul to Satan.

Here is one of the few instances in which romantics have attempted to embrace a bit of cultural context in reading a Johnson song. There's just one problem. Johnson was not singing, even indirectly, about a supernatural encounter. If the song is read at face value, it portrays the protagonist going to the crossroads in hopes of hitching a ride at sundown. True, the singer falls on his knees and asks the Lord to "save poor Bob if you please." But in the context of the song, this is not a plea for eternal salvation. Rather, the implicit terrors are more likely to be local white lawmen who often picked up musicians for vagrancy, or possibly night-riding bands of rednecks looking for an excuse to terrorize an African American.[11] In the second take Johnson's line "sun going down, boy, dark going to catch me here" calls up such old segregation-era signs as "Nigger, don't let the sun set on you here." Johnny Shines spoke vividly of the dangers African American musicians faced: "During the time back then, it was pretty unhealthy to be a musician, because you was not one that was known to work. And if you weren't known to be a work ox or slave labor, it was open season on you. Police could come and shoot you down and there was nothing said about it. There are people I've known for them to be killed in different places in the area, just for being there."[12]

We stop short of describing "Cross Road Blues" as social protest, partly because protest is not a recurrent theme in Johnson's repertoire and partly because protest songs were neither safe nor popular in the Deep South in that oppressive era. Samuel Charters nevertheless believed "Cross Road Blues" should be listed among songs devoted to social commentary and protest. He described the blues as a "reflection of the social restrictions which encircle the singer."[13]

As a final splash of cold water on the romanticized readings of "Cross Road Blues," note that most of the old folk beliefs are clear on at least one point: Anyone interested in a supernatural encounter would have to approach the crossroads in the middle of the night, not at sundown.[14]

Significantly, the version of "Cross Road Blues" that Vocalion marketed to African Americans in the thirties was not the version Frank Driggs chose to lead off the first Johnson reissue album in 1961. For one thing, the original version is more clearly addressed to a woman; Johnson calls out to her in all but the first verse as he describes his predicament. And the original concludes with the following verse: "I went to the crossroad, mama, I looked east and west, . . . Lord, I didn't have no sweet woman, ooh-well, babe, in my distress." Left alone, abandoned, or mistreated, he stands at the crossroad, looking this way and that for his woman. That verse clinches the underlying meaning: The original song was a plea for company, more likely to elicit sympathy from women in the audience than to traumatize them with visions of satanic pursuit.

Driggs, however, chose the unissued second take of "Cross Road Blues" as the first cut on side 1 of the 1961 LP. Whereas the first take contains six references indicating the song is addressed to a woman, the second contains but one, and it concludes not with the singer looking for his woman but with a reference to one of Johnson's earliest guitar influences: "You can run, you can run, tell my friend boy Willie Brown, . . . Lord, that I'm standing at the crossroad, babe, I believe I'm sinking down."

This is the version that set the tone for the way Johnson and his songs would be heard on the reissue album, a clear case of spin doctoring. Through liner notes and song selection, Driggs recast Johnson as a mystery man and loner, at odds with the supernatural rather than with the natural woman his traditional audience would have recognized. This recasting had everything to do with the perceived target audience. Driggs, as noted earlier, was editing the album to appeal to "folkies," the mainly young, mainly white consumers who had forsaken the insipid boy-girl themes in late-fifties rock and roll and doo-wop music to embrace the weightier themes of death, tragedy, spirituality, and politics found in some American folk music and the music associated with the labor, civil rights, and peace movements.

Here is a clear case of the shaping of Johnson's image not visually (as when the U.S. Postal Service deleted the cigarette from the photo portrait it used on a stamp) or critically (as when writers attempted to explain his songs) but musically, with Driggs acting as an A&R specialist, selecting and sequencing the takes in a way that best supported his own agenda. In this case the agenda was to present Johnson as a folk singer, alone and enigmatic, tormented by hideous inner phantoms.

✿

Johnson's fourth session, June 19, 1937, in Dallas, produced three songs: "Stones in My Passway," "I'm a Steady Rollin' Man," and "From Four until Late." Rock critic Greil Marcus said he found "Stones in My Passway" to be terrifying.[15] Well, it's true that "Stones in My Passway" presents the most extensive list of grievances of all Johnson's songs, but it ends with a traditional leaving verse and includes a typical seduction line, "I'm crying please, please let us be friends . . . rider, please open your door and let me in."

If any theme or pattern emerges from the output of the first four recording sessions, it is Johnson's way of calling attention to his own misfortunes and mistreatment. Most of these songs seem calculated to arouse sympathy and commiseration, not terror. Such songs were clearly part of Johnson's survival kit: On a good night they might persuade women in the audience to offer free lodging and other assistance of value to a walking musician.

Up to now we have seen little evidence of the supernatural, certainly nothing with which to construct a legend—nothing, that is, unless you count the inexplicable subtitle on "Preaching Blues" and the repeated references to standing at a crossroads in "Cross Road Blues." Now, however, we come to Johnson's final session, June 20, 1937, and things begin to heat up. During this marathon session he recorded, in this order, "Hellhound on My Trail," "Little Queen of Spades," "Malted Milk," "Drunken Hearted Man," "Me and the Devil Blues," "Stop Breaking Down Blues," "Traveling Riverside Blues," "Honeymoon Blues," "Love in Vain," and "Milkcow's Calf Blues."

Eight of these are standard blues fare. Both "Malted Milk" and "Drunken Hearted Man" are about booze, a common blues theme. "Malted Milk" makes a reference to "spooks" around the singer's bed, but in the context more of the DTs than of anything ghostly. Both pieces are played in a style derivative of Lonnie Johnson, and both portray the negative effects of drink. "Stop Breaking Down," a fairly typical sexual boast, later entered tradition through the version recorded by John Lee "Sonny Boy" Williamson. "Traveling Riverside Blues" revisits the "Rolling and Tumbling" theme and is an invitation to party. "Honeymoon Blues" is a love song done in almost a pop style. "Love in Vain" works the familiar train/separation theme. "Milkcow's Calf" is derivative of Kokomo Arnold's "Milk Cow Blues" (just as "Sweet Home Chicago," recorded at Johnson's first session in 1936, is derivative of Arnold's "Old Original Kokomo"). "Little Queen of Spades" uses gambling as a sexual metaphor and is reminiscent of ballads about gambling women such as Delia Holmes. The third verse refers to a mojo, a good-luck charm common in hoodoo folk beliefs. A mojo can make you lucky in gambling or in love. Interestingly, two days before Johnson hit town for his sessions, Texas piano player Harold Holiday, who recorded for Vocalion as Black Boy Shine, was in the same studio cutting such hoodoo-related numbers as "Gamblin' Jinx Blues" and "Brown Skin Mojo Blues." Did the two artists meet? No one knows. Did Don Law convey any ideas from the Holiday sessions to the Johnson sessions? Again, no one knows. But researcher David Evans wonders whether the two artists might have played together at some point. Their instrumental styles were "not incompatible," Evans says, and they both tended to portray themselves in song as restless characters involved in unstable relationships with women, with Johnson pursued by a hellhound while Holiday ran from poverty, police, and low-down mistreating women.[16] We argue that Johnson's hellhound was a metaphor for some of the same problems that beset Holiday.

While there is no hard evidence that Holiday ever played with Johnson, Holiday did play with the Texas artist J. T. "Funny Papa" Smith, with whom he recorded for Vocalion in Fort Worth in 1935. Both Holiday and, as we will soon show, Smith sang about the supernatural themes commonly associated with Johnson.

That brings us to the remaining two songs from the June 20 session, "Me and the Devil Blues" and "Hellhound on My Trail." These two became the big troublemakers, helping to seal Johnson's place in American music history for the worse, so let's take a closer look.

"Me and the Devil Blues"

"Me and the Devil Blues" is the only song Johnson recorded that makes explicit references to the devil and Satan, sustaining the devil or spirit theme through three of its four verses. Frank Driggs said the song offered evidence of the "weird, threatening monsters" that tormented Johnson.[17] David Evans said the song was Johnson's clearest indication of an "association with the devil."[18] Paul Oliver used the song in *Blues Fell This Morning* to comment on the dichotomy between blues and the Christian church,[19] and in his later book *The Story of the Blues,* he said the song exemplified the "angry utterances" and "obsessional . . . themes" that were strong indicators of a "paranoiac" personality in Johnson.[20]

Here again, listeners searching for evidence to support their favorite motif in the Johnson legend have pulled a song too far out of its context. The fact that there are no direct references to the devil or to Satan in any other Johnson song should have suggested to some of the critics and researchers that Johnson had no obsession with the supernatural and that an alternative reading of "Me and the Devil Blues" might be in order. Let us try to help.

The first verse opens with Johnson addressing someone or something: "Early this morning, when you knocked upon my door." This is a standard line in both blues and gospel songs. Sometimes it's the blues knocking on the door; sometimes it's the Grim Reaper. This time, it's Satan—or is it? In the overall context of the song, the singer could be addressing a woman; we've already seen how the devil became a blues cliché to explain a woman's faithless actions. In this instance, however, Johnson uses the term *Satan,* which calls attention to itself because it is not associated with the familiar "devil-got-my-woman" cliché. So maybe Johnson was addressing the personification of feelings of rage or jealously over something a woman did. This works even better in the context of the song, for in the next verse the devil and the singer are walking side by side as the latter contemplates beating his woman "until I get satisfied," which could mean until that devil rage is exorcised or, equally plausible, until he has beaten the devil out of his woman. (Keep in mind that in traditional blues, violence is often discussed, threatened, or considered but seldom carried out.)

The third verse shifts to the woman's perspective as she wonders why he is so suspicious of her and offers the excuse that "it must be that old evil spirit so deep down in the ground."[21] Also in this verse he comes right out and tells her (and us) why he is thinking of resorting to mayhem when, in a spoken aside, he says, "Now, babe, you know you ain't doing me right, don't you?"

In the final verse Johnson makes it clear to his woman that he feels no remorse and couldn't care less about the destination of his soul for eternity. When he dies, he sings, just bury him "down by the highway side, so my old evil spirit can catch a Greyhound bus and ride." And he underscores the unrepentant tone with another spoken aside: "Baby, I don't care where you bury my body when I'm dead and gone."

In this interpretation, which we argue is more in line with the content of Johnson's other recorded blues, it's not a song about possession or paranoia. Nor is it a window into the supernatural beliefs of the singer. It is a song about the suspicions and jealousies that can erupt in romantic relationships. Given the remorseless, almost boastful, tone of Johnson's verses, and considering all the blues containing similar sarcastic or comic burial instructions, the song was solidly in touch with tradition. It must have elicited raucous responses from Johnson's jook-house audiences.[22]

While none of the critics or researchers has yet written that "Me and the Devil Blues" sounds scary, that can't be said of "Hellhound on My Trail."

"Hellhound on My Trail"

After Skip James recorded "Devil Got My Woman" for Paramount in 1931, several other artists produced songs that were clearly influenced by James's unusual style. Two bear mention here: Joe McCoy, an artist from Jackson, Mississippi, recorded "Evil Devil Woman Blues" for Decca in 1934, and Johnnie Temple, also from Jackson, cut "The Evil Devil Blues" in 1935 for Vocalion. By most accounts Johnson played in Jackson in 1931 and 1932, and Stephen Calt believes that Johnson learned Temple's piece when the two met there. This supposition gains plausibility when you hear Temple using what sounds like Johnson's walking bass figure on "Lead Pencil Blues," recorded at the same session as "The Evil Devil Blues."[23] Johnson recorded "Hellhound" for Vocalion, the same label that recorded Temple, two years after Temple's session. Establishing a definite connection between Johnson and McCoy is more difficult. But the point is that several musicians were employing James's mournful-sounding minor-key style to sing about subjects linked to the devil.

In his song James uses the devil in two ways: first, as a hypothetical comparison to illustrate the enormity of his misfortune—"I'd rather be the devil than be my woman's man"—and second, as an explanation for the misfortune—"Because nothing but the devil changed my baby's mind." This idea, that the devil must have been behind a woman's hurtful actions, shows up in countless blues. McCoy's run at the devil theme is similar: "I'd rather be the devil than be my woman's man . . . Oh, she was evil, wouldn't work hand in hand." Temple's version follows suit, but with a morbid twist: "I'd rather be dead and in my horrible tomb . . . To hear my woman, some man done taken my room." Temple also echoes James with lines such as this one: "I'd rather be the devil than be that woman's man . . . The devil's evil, changed my baby's mind." So there was a pattern, using the image of the devil to contrast, describe, or scapegoat the shifts and tensions that inevitably arise in romantic relationships.

But Johnson's lyrics in "Hellhound" move in a new and singular direction. He uses the hellhound and other powerful images to describe an internal conflict between compulsive wanderlust and longing for the ideal of staying put with a woman. In the first verse, which is the only one to mention the hellhound, he gives us a weather metaphor to describe the urgency of rambling: "I got to keep moving, blues falling down like hail. . . . And the days keep on worrying me, there's a hellhound on my trail."[24] The second verse paints an upbeat picture of rest and togetherness in the company of a woman, with Christmas Eve and Christmas Day as a homey backdrop. The third verse starts with a hoodoo reference and returns to images of motion and travel, only now it is the actions of a woman, not the hellhound, that keep the singer on the move: "You sprinkled hot-foot powder all around your daddy's door, . . . It keep me with a rambling mind, rider, every old place I go." The last verse returns to ominous weather imagery—wind rising and leaves trembling—and then concludes: "All I need's my sweet little woman to keep my company." So when all is said and done, we're back to seduction.

While the hellhound is not widely used in blues idiom, it is a recognized feature in African American folk belief, along with dog ghosts, hounds from hell, and dogs with blazing eyes. The use of dogs to chase runaways—convicts or slaves—could easily have added to the image's potency. In any case, scholars familiar with blues lyrics have noted several prior usages of the hellhound image. For example, Kentuckian Sylvester Weaver's 1927 recording of "Devil Blues" contains this verse: "Hellhounds start to chase me, man, I was a running fool. My ankles caught on fire, couldn't keep my puppies cool." And in 1931 the Texas bluesman J. T. "Funny Papa" Smith recorded "Howling Wolf Blues No. 3," which included these lines: "I take time when I'm out prowling, and wipe out my tracks with my tail. . . . Get home and get blue and start howling, and the hellhound get on my trail." In these earlier blues the tone is either comic or more in line with sexual boasting.

Johnson's "Hellhound" is none of that. It is blues poem about the driven nature of the walking musician's travels and the fleeting nature of his relationships with women. But why is "Hellhound" regarded with such awe? Why has it been invested with so much mystery and endlessly probed for answers to Johnson's life and personality?

Here is the likely answer: "Hellhound" isn't like Johnson's other recorded songs. It sounds, for lack of a better phrase, a little spooky. It sounded strange even to people who'd been close to Johnson, according to Mack McCormick. McCormick reported that when he played a recording of the song for Johnson's family members or friends, they'd say, "That sounds like Robert's voice, but it couldn't be him. He wouldn't sing anything like that. Robert was just a sweet, ordinary person."[25]

Even keeping in mind that Johnson played—spectacularly well—in a variety of styles, "Hellhound" still stands in sharp contrast to the more familiar styles in his repertoire. But this is not a big mystery. As already demonstrated, "Hellhound" was inspired by songs such as McCoy's "Evil Devil Woman Blues" and Temple's "Evil Devil Blues," which in turn were based on "Devil Got My Woman," by Bentonia's Skip James. James played in an open minor tuning, which was unusual in that day, and sang in a plaintive falsetto, also unusual. James's sound has been characterized as spooky, eerie, and weird (as has the music of his fellow Bentonia bluesman Jack Owens). It should come as no surprise, then, that Johnson's attempt to emulate the Bentonia style—if there is such a thing—would incorporate those same qualities. Yet what is considered typical of James is regarded as unique and portentous when done by Johnson.

Thus here is the final irony: In "Hellhound" Johnson is performing in a style unrepresentative of his work in general, yet this song has been selected, not by his down-home audience or his fellow musicians but by the literary-based critical establishment, as the one song that best represents who he was and what he did.

❋

Before leaving "Hellhound," let's return to the blues of J. T. "Funny Papa" Smith, who scored several hits for Vocalion in the early thirties while employing the persona of "the Howling Wolf." As already noted, Smith, too, sang of having a hellhound on his trail—that being but one of several striking similarities to images in some of Johnson's songs. Take, for example, the word *howling,* which can be a phonetic rendering of *hollering,* a common blues term. Johnson uses it in two songs recorded back to back on June 19, 1937. In "Stones in My Passway" he sings, "and when you hear me howling in my passway, rider, please open your door and let me in." And in "Steady Rolling Man" he sings: "and when you hear me howling, baby, umm, down on my bended knee." Seven years earlier, in "Howlin Wolf Blues No. 2," Smith sang, "Now when you hear howling, mama, I mean howling at your door" and, in another verse, "Baby, here I am down on my bending knee." Johnson's "Stones in My Passway" includes the line, "I got stones in my passway, and my road seems dark as night." Earlier, Smith sang, "watch the road's dark as night and you're liable to see me prowl."

Smith's lyrics sometimes make Johnson's seem benign. Here's a sample from "Hungry Wolf Blues," recorded for Vocalion in 1931: "I stroll through dark places threatening to do my part, with blood in my eye and malice in my heart." What is more, Smith, like the legendary Faust, felt as though he had fallen out of favor with the man upstairs: "Look like God don't treat me like I'm a human kind . . . Seems like He wants me to be a prowler and a howling wolf all the time." Smith also recorded an extensive reference to hoodoo magic in his two-part 1931 tribute to divination, "Seven Sisters Blues." Yet no one has ever suggested that Smith must have cut a deal with the devil.

When Smith was recording his Howling Wolf sides for Vocalion, Don Law had not yet become an A&R supervisor but was working as a record sales manager. In June 1931, six months after Smith had recorded his "Howling Wolf Blues No. 3," with the phrase "hellhound get on my trail," Law wrote a promotional letter to Vocalion's retailers plugging the side: "Remember Howling Wolf Blues is the biggest selling record on the market today."[26]

Fast forward to 1937. Having scored a regional hit with Smith's blues, did Law bounce a couple of ideas off Johnson in the hopes of scoring again with a similar song? Was Johnson already familiar with Smith's music, and had he applied his musical sponge to some of Smith's lyrics? We will never know. About all we can say for sure is that Johnson's songs contained a number of images and phrases that were remarkably similar to Smith's, and that Don Law was somehow involved in the mix.

For over fifty years one stubborn belief supported the master-detective approach to Johnson's song texts. It was a belief that Johnson's songs were a reflection of his life, particularly his inner life. But that belief weakens when the songs are examined in the context of Johnson's culture. While snatches of autobiography may show up in some of Johnson's songs, the words and music are much more a reflection of blues tradition, African American vernacular, and Johnson's well-honed talents as an artist and showman.

Taken individually or as a group, the twenty-nine recorded songs offer no verifiable information on which to base a claim that Johnson was paranoiac, tormented, self-destructive, disillusioned, or any of the other dark characterizations that have been put forward since Rudi Blesh first wrote that "Hellhound on My Trail" evoked images "full of evil, surcharged with the terror of one alone among the moving, unseen shapes of the night."[27] It would be just as easy—and just as misguided—to cull the song texts for "proof" that Johnson was loving and kind, or a closet Christian, or a conjurer, or some other fanciful depiction.

Nor do the song texts offer evidentiary support for claims that Johnson believed he had sold his soul to the devil, that he was "drawn to the texture" of being in league with Satan, or that he encouraged people around him to believe that he had made a pact with the devil. But that hasn't stopped the detectives—fans and researchers alike—from looking elsewhere for evidence to prop up the Faustian motif in Johnson's biography. So let's examine the evidence they've compiled.

12 A House of Cards

It's so stupid to sit and talk about these things—white people don't know a fucking thing.

— Ry Cooder, quoted in Tony Scherman, "The Hellhound's Trail"

Because Johnson's own songs inspired so much speculation about a supernatural connection, legend sleuths have always been on the lookout for hard historical evidence of a link between the artist and old folk beliefs about voodoo, hoodoo, and "the devil's music." Such evidence, while not abundant, does exist in the "oral histories" of people such as Willie Mae Powell, Queen Elizabeth, and David "Honeyboy" Edwards, as we have seen. But have the legend sleuths been constructing a case based on evidence or constructing evidence based on a case?

The answer will be clear, we believe, if we go back and trace the historical development. This path leads back to a single essay, "Hell Hound on His Trail: Robert Johnson," written by the jazz critic Pete Welding, published in 1966 by *Down Beat* magazine, and later reprinted in the British journal *Blues Unlimited.* In the book *Chasin' That Devil Music* the researchers Gayle Dean Wardlow and Edward Komara identify the Welding essay as the start of all the Faustian mythology; they pinpoint a partial quote attributed to Johnson's early mentor Son House as the first explicit suggestion of a

deal between Johnson and Satan.[1] From House's quote, the trail of incrim-
inating references leads to a David Evans interview with the brother of the
blues artist Tommy Johnson and then to a Greil Marcus commentary in the
book *Mystery Train,* Peter Guralnick's short biography *Searching for Robert
Johnson,* Robert Palmer's book *Deep Blues,* and the Hollywood feature film
Crossroads. Wardlow and Komara do a fine job of exposing these references as leaps of faith, speculation, insinuation, obliging responses to leading questions, or pure fiction.[2]

To the Wardlow-Komara list we suggest adding at least two other ref-
erences that have been used to bolster the supernatural case against
Johnson: first, Johnny Shines's statement that he heard "black arts" might
have been involved in Johnson's death, and second, the full telling of
Son House's colorful but inaccurate recollection regarding how quickly
Johnson mastered blues guitar.

The House recollection helped set the stage for all the legend making that came afterward. It first appeared as part of a lengthy interview
done by Julius Lester and published in *Sing Out!* magazine in 1965. As
noted in chapter 7, House's story, in the version told to Lester, provided
indirect corroboration to the dark side of the Johnson legend through a
link to old folk beliefs about secular music—specifically the belief that
you could become a blues musician, virtually overnight, if you were willing to relinquish your soul to the devil. The key phrase there is "indirect
corroboration," as we will soon show. Samuel Charters and Peter Guralnick
were among the blues researchers who later incorporated portions of
House's story into their biographies of Johnson. Pete Welding also quoted the House recollection in his 1966 essay, although his version differs—
slightly yet significantly—from the one that appeared in *Sing Out!* magazine. More recently a portion of Son House's story turned up in Sherman
Alexie's novel *Reservation Blues.*

Because of the centrality of the devil deal in Johnson's biographical
reconstruction, let's revisit the case made by Wardlow. And let's begin with
the 1966 Welding essay. As a prelude to the dark suggestion of a devil deal,
Welding offered a version of Son House's recollection of the speed with
which young Johnson advanced from bad to brilliant as a guitar player.
In the familiar story line Robert annoys people at parties by trying to play
guitars that belong to House and Willie Brown; then, after Robert runs

away from home, he returns just "six or seven months later," confronts House and Brown at a dance, and asks them to let him play. As quoted in the Welding essay, House recalled:

> "We gets up, you know—laughs at him. So he sets down and he starts playing, and when he got through, all our mouths was open. . . . yeah, what happened was a big surprise—how he did it that fast."
>
> . . . House suggested in all seriousness that Johnson, in his months away from home, had "sold his soul to the devil in exchange for learning to play like that."[3]

That final sentence, just twenty-eight words long, was the seed that grew into a legend, according to Wardlow and Komara. Expanding on their findings, we find the sentence troublesome on at least four counts:

First, the concluding remark from House is only a partial quote, so the original context cannot be divined by the reader. Was there something in the original context that caused Welding to write "House suggested" instead of "House claimed" or the simpler and more direct "House said"?

Second, Welding did not identify a source for the devil quote or any of the other extensive quotes attributed to House, which implies that Welding himself interviewed House. The prolific Welding did publish interviews with at least ten blues musicians, but he never published a full interview with House, and no tape or transcript of an interview with House has surfaced since Welding's death.

Third, for anyone who has read verbatim transcripts of interviews with House (see chapter 6, note 12) or listened to recordings of interviews, the phrasing of the partial quote seems stilted in comparison to House's normal speech cadences.

Fourth, if House did speak those words exactly as Welding wrote them, it was the only time House said any such thing. In the Lester interview published in *Sing Out!* some months before Welding's essay, House spoke at length about Johnson's rapid development as a guitar player but never said anything about the devil's getting involved. And he remained a reluctant witness, at best, for those who later sought testimony implicating Johnson in a satanic bargain. Dick Waterman, who helped revive House's career in the sixties, said he never once heard House say anything about a devil deal. Ed Komara said House was sometimes asked by Waterman about Johnson's supposed deal with Satan and always dismissed the idea.[4] Paul Vernon, who along with Bengt Ollson interviewed House in the late 1960s, said that when they asked about the Johnson legend, House said, "I don't want to talk about that," remaining silent until the questioning moved to another subject.[5] It is remarkable, to say the least, that House would say something to Welding that he steadfastly refused to repeat ever again.

The Welding version of House's story differs from the Lester version on a number of small points. In the Welding version, for example, Johnson returns to Robinsonville carrying a guitar strung with seven strings instead of the standard six.[6] In the Lester interview strings aren't mentioned. In the Welding version House remembered Johnson living on Pope's plantation. In the Lester version House remembered that Johnson was living with his stepfather on a plantation owned by a man named "Richard Lellman." (Samuel Charters, traveling in the Robinsonville area later, found signs for a farm owned by R. Leatherman and concluded that it must have been the place House remembered.)

The Welding version further differs on one possibly salient detail besides the damning partial quote about a devil deal. The Welding version quotes House as saying the surprising thing about Johnson was "how he did it that fast."[7] In the Lester interview House recalled making the comment to Willie Brown, "Well, ain't that fast!"[8] Perhaps we attach too much significance to a small detail, but House seemed to be telling Lester that what made Johnson "so good" was his ability to play up-tempo—fast— the same ability that impressed many of Johnson's other contemporaries. In the Welding account House seemed to be impressed instead by the speed with which Johnson learned, a variation that conveniently (or coincidentally) dovetailed with old folk beliefs about learning the "devil's music."

Was the variation caused by a transcription error? Is it possible that Welding did interview House but misunderstood what House meant when he used the word *fast* in relation to Johnson's playing? And if he did misunderstand, is it possible that he felt it would be permissible to embellish House's account with an out-of-context quote—or one derived from one of his own interview questions—implicating Johnson in a trade with Old Nick? Although we don't have access to a tape of the Welding interview of House, assuming there was one, a Welding interview with David "Honeyboy" Edwards, one of Johnson's friends, was recently put out on a CD recording.[9] A comparison of the CD to a 1971 print transcript of the same interview provides insight into Welding's methodology.[10] In the recorded interview Welding steers his subject with rapid-fire questions, some of them clearly leading—an approach typical of journalists and field researchers seeking maximum information on an often limited supply of tape. But the approach lends itself to shaping what the interview subject has to say or even how the subject says it. To take one example, when Welding asks, "Did you hear him play a lot?" Edwards answers, "Yeah." In the printed transcript Edwards is quoted as saying, "I heard him play a lot," with no trace of Welding's question. Putting words into other people's mouths is common enough among journalists trying to corroborate information, but the practice creates a dilemma for the reader. Without seeing the questions, the reader has no way of knowing whether the information between quotation marks was offered or extracted, complete or partial, or even uttered at all. To compound this dilemma, parts of the Edwards interview were moved around in the transcript, and some of what Edwards said was incorrectly transcribed. Regardless of whether Welding or someone else did the transcription, the result raises questions about methodology and casts additional doubt on the Welding version of House's recollection.

While the Welding version contained what is believed to be the first explicit suggestion of a deal between Robert Johnson and the devil, this source was seldom mentioned by later writers who expanded on the legend. One notable exception was rock critic Greil Marcus, who cited Welding by name in the 1975 book *Mystery Train*. Marcus presented the damning quote from House as a complete sentence, however, not a fragment, and with slightly altered wording: "'He sold his soul to the devil to get to play like that,' House told Welding."[11] This wording was certainly less stilted than the wording in Welding's essay, but one wonders why the quote was reworded (assuming that's what was done). Isn't a quote supposed to provide the exact phrasing of a spoken or written passage? It's a nitpicky point, but a potentially significant one, because it touches, again, on the issue of methodology—in this case, Marcus's. *Mystery Train* was regarded as an important book in its day, and the chapter on Johnson offered the first extended argument that the artist believed his soul belonged to Satan. Marcus asserted that "selling his soul and trying to win it back are what Johnson's bravest songs are all about."[12] And what sort of evidence, other than the refurbished and highly dubious quote from Son House, did Marcus present for this view of Johnson? "Let us say," Marcus suggested at one point, "that Johnson sought out one of the Mississippi Delta devil men or devil women and tried to sell his soul."[13] The influence of this kind of glib speculation on Marcus's contemporaries cannot be calculated with any precision, but it is worth noting that most of the literature and pop-culture documents linking Johnson to a devil deal were produced after *Mystery Train*.

Let's return briefly to the Marcus variation on Welding's quote fragment. The reworded quote from Son House turned up most recently in a 1997 book by the British writer Tony Russell, who gave the words an interesting new spin: "[Johnson] returned to Hazlehurst for a year or two, and when he came back to Robinsonville he showed the older men how he'd improved. 'When he got through,' House remembered, 'all our mouths was open.' He would sometimes add, 'He sold his soul to the devil to get to play like that.'"[14] We asked Russell to identify his source for the assertion that House "would sometimes add" words he is believed to have uttered only once, if that. Russell said he was unable to locate the source.[15]

The most influential and oft-quoted testimony concerning a fateful crossroads connection with the devil came from a 1966 interview that David Evans did with the bluesman-turned-preacher LeDell Johnson, brother of the blues artist Tommy Johnson. LeDell described in great detail how a shadowy figure emerged from the crossroads darkness late at night and retuned the guitar of the musician waiting there, thus conferring the ability to play any song the musician might wish but also taking possession of the musician's soul. There was just one huge problem with LeDell's vivid story: He was recounting how his brother Tommy supposedly had sold *his* soul to the devil; the story had nothing to do with Robert Johnson. Yet it eventually became more closely associated with Robert Johnson than with Tommy Johnson. This was evident as late as 1999, when the French writer Jean-Paul Levet, in an essay published in *Soul Bag*, repeated the

LeDell Johnson story about Tommy Johnson, but with one small parenthetical addition at the beginning of the quote, indicated here in italics: "He (*Robert Johnson*) said the reason he knowed so much, said he sold hisself to the devil."[16] In 1989 LeDell's story showed up in Guralnick's biography of Robert Johnson. Unlike Levet, Guralnick got the story right, putting Tommy Johnson, not our Robert, at the crossroads to make a midnight deal with the devil. But Guralnick gave the story a Welding-like spin, confidently reporting, "Son House was convinced that Robert Johnson had done the same thing."[17]

Interviewed by Pearson in 1993, Evans said he was at a loss to explain how LeDell's testimony about Tommy Johnson got mixed up in the Robert Johnson legend. Evans also said that LeDell's testimony included two other fascinating claims, namely, that he'd seen a white woman give birth to the devil's baby and had once been attacked by a winged serpent when he was out riding a bicycle. It is apparent from such accounts that anything we hear from LeDell should be taken with a grain of salt, as Evans himself suggested during the 1993 interview. Further weakening LeDell's credibility is a pre-1967 interview with Gayle Wardlow during which LeDell made no mention of the devil's having taken possession of his brother's soul in a trade for talent. He claimed instead that he, LeDell, had been Tommy's musical mentor: "I learned Tommy how to play the guitar first . . . long before he ran away from home."[18] It is also worth noting that Tommy Johnson's other brother, Mager, was furious with LeDell for telling the crossroads story, which he felt was a slander.[19]

Next the paper trail moves to Robert Palmer. He constructs his Faustian case on equally tenuous foundations, citing unnamed sources who allegedly told researcher Mack McCormick, who then told Palmer, that Johnson sold his soul to the devil: "'The devil came there,' said one [of the unnamed sources], 'and gave Robert his talent and told him he had eight more years to live on earth.'"[20]

The mysterious sources were supposedly related to Johnson, but who were they? And how did what is presented as a direct quote get from McCormick to Palmer? It's all a little vague, which raises questions once again about methodology. It also underscores a continuing problem: McCormick, who is an important source for writers such as Palmer and Guralnick and for the film *The Search for Robert Johnson,* hasn't been willing to name names when it comes to his sources. Perhaps he will do so, as we noted earlier, when *Biography of a Phantom* hits the presses or when the sources are dead and buried. But until then, we are left in the dark.

Palmer goes on to speculate that Robert Johnson "certainly" had heard of Tommy Johnson, his rabbit-foot charm, and his supposed covenant with Satan. We're not so certain about that; it is reasonable to suppose that Robert Johnson had heard of Tommy Johnson but far less certain that Robert had heard about any deal with the devil. That's because Tommy's deal is another one of the great unsupported assumptions in blues lore. There is no testimony from any of Tommy's contemporaries indicating that Tommy portrayed himself as having bartered his soul at a crossroads. That story originated with LeDell long after Tommy Johnson and Robert Johnson were dead. Anyway, Palmer continues to build his case by bringing in the previously cited anecdote about a friend's scary experience at a Delta crossroads (see chapter 7) and citing hearsay that Robert Johnson's musical mentor, Ike Zinnerman, learned to play by visiting graveyards at midnight. In sum, Palmer employs a third-hand quote, a leap of unsupported speculation, some hearsay, and an anecdote about something that happened to a friend to suggest that Robert Johnson may have had a dark little secret. In this way Palmer's widely read and influential book comes down on the pro side—at least by implication—of the devil-deal controversy.

Having already discussed the Faustian theme in the 1986 film *Crossroads* (see chapter 8), we will add only that the movie's story line roughly parallels a sixth-century Anatolian narrative in which a clergyman gains power by selling himself to Satan but manages to get off the hook thanks to the intervention of the Virgin Mary—whose soul-saving role is played by fresh-faced Ralph Macchio in the film.

Whether the ending was happy or tragic, the Faust story was deeply embedded in English literary tradition. When brought to the New World, the story became a mainstay of American popular culture. It appears in literature, such as Stephen Vincent Benet's novel *The Devil and Daniel Webster;* art; animated cartoons; movies; and even a Broadway musical, *Damn Yankees.* The story also became woven into American folklore, in part because the motif of the diabolical bargain meshed with folk beliefs about the sinful nature of secular music and dance. Certain dance-related instruments—mainly the fiddle, banjo, and guitar—became known as the devil's instruments or the devil's boxes. In addition, stories about selling one's soul in exchange for musical talent, luck in gambling, or some other gift were common in African American folk tradition dating from at least the nineteenth century. While working in the deep South in the twenties, the folklorist Newbell Niles "Barry" Puckett collected a number of such stories, including one attributed to a New Orleans conjurer who suggested the following sequence for aspiring guitar players:

First, he counseled, trim your nails as close as possible, and then, at midnight, take your guitar to a lonely fork in the road and begin playing your best piece—all the while wishing for the devil to appear. You will hear, but not see, a guitar player who will sit down next to you, swap his guitar for yours, and play along with you. When the unseen musician stops playing, he will trim your nails until they bleed and then hand back your guitar, which you must continue playing without looking around. At that point, the conjurer told Puckett, your deal with the devil will be sealed, and you will be able to play whatever you want.[21]

Harry M. Hyatt, an Episcopal rector who collected folk tales, published seventy-three examples of similar stories, which he heard between 1936 and 1940 in North and South Carolina, Virginia, and Maryland.[22] Hyatt's examples fall basically into two categories: "how to" instructions on selling one's soul, similar to the Puckett example, and legends about people who attempted the fateful negotiation—most of whom lost their nerve and ran away, underscoring a traditional function of such stories as lessons in what not to do.

Cecelia Conway, a folklorist, published a more current example told by the North Carolina guitarist Willie Trice in the seventies. Trice said his uncle had gone to the crossroads to learn banjo from the devil but was frightened by an apparition with bright red eyes and balls of fire coming out of its mouth. In language typical of the legend, Trice declared "he couldn't stand it and ran on home."[23]

It is not unreasonable to assume that Robert Johnson heard similar folk stories from family members or playmates when he was growing up. But it is a long and perilous jump from that assumption to a conclusion that Johnson either sold his soul to the devil or consciously encouraged the belief that he had.

Until his own death in 1992, Johnny Shines was Robert Johnson's staunch-est defender. Shines left no question that he considered any soul-selling story a slander against the musician with whom he once traveled and performed. So it is particularly ironic that a phrase attributed to Shines has been used to bolster the link between Johnson and supernatural beliefs. The phrase first turned up in the same 1966 Pete Welding essay that sup-posedly gave birth to the crossroads mythology. In the essay Shines re-called hearing the news that Johnson was dead, poisoned "by one of those women who really didn't care for him." The quote continued: "That was down in Eudora, Miss., that it happened. And I heard that it was something to do with the black arts. Before he died, it was said, Robert was crawl-ing along the ground on all fours, barking and snapping like a mad beast. That's what the poison done to him."[24]

A reference to "black arts" also turned up in Samuel Charters's short biography of Johnson in 1973, and the phrase was again attributed to Shines. Charters did not say he pulled the phrase from Welding's essay, so we assume that he heard it from Shines himself.

While the phrase "black arts" was recycled in a number of written ac-counts of Johnson's death, Shines did not use it again in any interview published after 1970. In a long interview with Welding that was published in 1975, for example, Shines again said he'd heard that the dying John-son crawled on hands and knees and barked like a dog. And Shines re-peated the story that Johnson had died in the arms of the harp player Sonny Boy Williamson no. 2 but made no reference to "black arts." In that interview Shines also switched the scene of Johnson's death from Eudo-ra to Meridian, Mississippi, even though researchers by then had nar-rowed the scene to the Greenwood area. This could be an indication that Shines was still relying mainly on the musicians' grapevine for informa-tion. Indeed, Shines always said that most of what he knew, or thought he knew, about Johnson's death originally came from Williamson: "The only time I paid very much attention to Robert being dead was after I met Sonny Boy. . . . I ran upon him—I think this was long about 1940—and he was telling me for certain that he was dead. He died in his arms. So then I began to kind of believe it. But later on I found out that he was such a big liar."[25]

Beyond the paper trail examined by Wardlow and Komara, we find several other comments that might be construed as evidence against Johnson. One of them came from the blues artist Bukka White during an unpublished conversation with Al Young, a musician and writer. Recalling the stories about Johnson's rapid acquisition of musical talent, White reportedly told Young, "Now you mean to tell me he ain't made some kind of deal with the devil?" Young felt the comment was "more hearsay than daresay," since White had never met Johnson.[26] White never repeated his rhetorical question in any of the published interviews with him.

It's conceivable that White was simply repeating something he had picked up from another interviewer, since revival artists were routinely barraged with questions about Johnson—so much so that the interviews became irksome. Johnny Shines, for example, grew tired of talking about someone other than himself. House and White, too, were reported to have resented the focus on Johnson at the expense of their own considerable prowess as bluesmen.

The blues-record collector Michael Leonard claimed he was told by a man named Walter Hearns in Greenwood, Mississippi, that Johnson had made a deal with the devil in a graveyard. Hearns supposedly said that Johnson had spent the night in a graveyard, and when he came out the next morning, he walked down the street playing "Preaching Blues," followed by Hearns and several friends, who were still children at the time. To add mystery to this account, Leonard said that when he went back to get the story on tape, he learned that Hearns was dead.[27]

When Robert's former girlfriend Willie Mae Powell said "it's the truth" that Johnson "sold himself" at the crossroads, she said she got the story not from Johnson himself but from her cousin, David "Honeyboy" Edwards (see chapter 8). It appears, however, that Edwards did not become a source of information on Johnson's crossroads connection until the late eighties or early nineties—a period that coincided with the release of the movie *Crossroads,* the spasm of romantic hype brought on by the CD of Johnson's complete recordings, and a report that famed director Martin Scorsese was interested in filming a script based on the Johnson legend. What's more, Edwards often seemed of two minds on Johnson's supposed deal with the devil, in one breath indicating that he had heard the crossroads legend from other people and in the next breath hinting that he might have heard it from Johnson himself. At blues festivals Edwards most often discussed the crossroads in the context of old folk beliefs and superstitions that he and (probably) Johnson heard when they were growing up.[28] Edwards said he played his guitar late at night at a crossroads at least once in the belief that it might help him become a better musician, although he never expected to meet the devil there and never believed it was possible to sell one's self to the devil. Edwards said he also carried a bag of dried scorpions in his pocket as a good-luck charm and hung a guitar over his bed to see if he would become a better player. As for Johnson, said Edwards in his 1997 autobiography, he might have believed it was possible to cut a deal with the devil: "he could have felt that he sold his soul."[29] Was Edwards suggesting that Johnson told him something along this line, or was he simply acknowledging the story line that had emerged in the early nineties?

One of Johnson's friends from the Robinsonville years, Willie Coffee, recalled hearing Johnson saying that he had sold his soul to the devil. The context for the comment, which was made during a filmed interview with Stephen LaVere, was a brief rumination on the question of how Johnson had become a stellar guitar player so quickly. It wasn't clear, however, whether Coffee or LaVere had brought up the story of Johnson's rapid development, because the film omitted the lead-in question, if there was one. In any case, LaVere went on to ask Coffee if he ever really believed Johnson's claim that he had sold his soul, and Coffee replied, in part, "I never did believe it."[30]

LaVere, in fairness, seems to be one of the people least likely to solicit a comment about Johnson's rapid development as a guitar player, because he knew from his own research how and from whom Johnson learned to play. LaVere knew it did not happen overnight or even in six months. It was an entirely earthly process that probably occurred over a period of years: Johnson first learned on his homemade diddley bow, possibly picking up some rudimentary chords from one of his brothers, and later became a serious student when he was exposed to the playing of House, Brown, Zinnerman (or possibly the Zinnerman brothers), and anyone else who had a song or a guitar riff he liked. House and other contemporaries said Johnson learned by listening and paying attention to each player's fingering—the same method, incidentally, by which he became a proficient pianist. As secretive as he was about his own chords and techniques, he could be an inquisitive pest when trying to absorb another musician's techniques. In sum, the more closely we examine the Johnson crossroads legend, the more chimerical it becomes.

Three years after the filmed interview with Coffee was released, LaVere was asked why he had asked a question about a devil deal. He said he had posed the question solely in the interest of debunking the crossroads legend.[31] LaVere said he thought Coffee's response accomplished that purpose, noting that Coffee went on to say he would have dismissed any soul-selling claims by Johnson as "a lot of jive" because Johnson was always joking around.

Before heading into final arguments, let's summarize all the evidence—from earlier chapters as well as this one—linking Robert Johnson to a Faustian bargain or some other supernatural connection. Let's see how much of the evidence would stand up, say, in a court of law:

Son House: He implicated Johnson in a partial quote, fourteen words long, that appeared in a 1966 essay. The quote conveyed an idea that House either repudiated or refused to repeat in all subsequent interviews. Was the quote legitimate? Not beyond a reasonable doubt.

LeDell Johnson: His dramatic crossroads story, repeated in at least two biographical sketches of Robert Johnson, had nothing to do with Robert Johnson. The testimony was irrelevant.

Greil Marcus: His suggestion that Johnson might have gone to see one of the Delta's "devil men or devil women" came right out of Marcus's own imagination, as did Marcus's portrait of Johnson as a man who believed his soul belonged to Satan. The jury shall disregard both.

Robert Palmer: His book *Deep Blues* contained a single quote from an unidentified source, an unsupported assumption, a bit of hearsay about one of Johnson's guitar mentors, and a chilling account of what Johnson might have imagined had he gone to the crossroads in the middle of the night and heard strange noises in the distance. We think the judge would instruct the jury to disregard this highly speculative testimony.

Crossroads: This Hollywood treatment of the crossroads legend offered some interesting music and a few authentic Delta touches, but the film, mostly a vehicle for a teen star, was accurately described by movie reviewers as formulaic fluff.

William Barlow: In his 1989 book about blues culture, he claimed that Johnson was "known to have encouraged the legend that he made a pact with Satan." This is pure invention.

Mack McCormick: His assertion, captured in a 1993 film, that Johnson consciously adopted a "me-and-the-devil" persona has never been supported by the findings of any other researcher. Until McCormick comes up with more documentation, the testimony must be regarded as dubious.

Alan Lomax: He said that he met Robert Johnson's mother in 1942 and that she told him that Robert, in a deathbed declaration, had renounced the guitar, referring to it as "the devil's instrument." We have already catalogued the problems with this account, among them the mother's name, the fact that no one else ever uncovered evidence of a maternal visit to Johnson's deathbed, and the five decades Lomax waited before describing the encounter. A reasonable jury, we believe, would find the account too full of holes to be credible.

Bukka White: His rhetorical question, made in the course of a conversation, was never published but was passed along by someone else. In a court of law that qualifies as hearsay.

Walter Hearns: The tale he told before his death was never documented. Again, it's hearsay.

Honeyboy Edwards: He didn't remember (or at least he didn't mention) the crossroads legend until it became a part of the pop-culture iconography surrounding Johnson.

Johnson's former girlfriends: Willie Mae Powell says she heard about the crossroads deal not from Johnson but from Honeyboy Edwards. Her testimony on this subject is hearsay. But the jury may want to consider her firsthand impression of Johnson: "He was a nice-conditioned person. He was loving and kind."[32] Queen Elizabeth's testimony is sketchy, at best, and tainted by the fervor of her negative feelings about blues, blues singers, and Johnson.

Willie Coffee: In a filmed interview with Stephen LaVere, Coffee said he would have laughed off any soul-selling claims by Johnson because

Johnson was such a jokester. LaVere says he believes that Coffee was an effective debunker.

Lost evidence, missing interviews, faulty attribution, hearsay, colorful testimony: Will it ever be sorted out? Sadly, the trail we've been following has gone cold. House is dead. Lomax, Welding, White, and Shines are gone, too. The year before he died, however, Shines participated in the Smithsonian Institution's Folklife Festival program "The Roots of Rhythm and Blues: A Tribute to the Robert Johnson Era." During one festival workshop, as in various films and interviews, he ridiculed the Johnson legend:

> I tell you, I want anybody that believes in that, bring me your soul up here and lay it on the stage. I want to see it. If you can sell your soul you got to have control over it. Anything that you can sell or trade, you have to control. So if you have control over your soul, bring it up here and lay it on the stage. If you can't do that, you can't sell your soul. I don't believe in those lies. . . . I never did believe it. There's a whole lot of stuff I used to hear when I was a kid. I was glad when I got big enough to get the heck out of the house so I wouldn't have to hear any more of that stuff. . . . I mean, my daddy was well educated but he believed that stuff because he talked it to me—about a bear meeting you in the road with a twig and beat you to death. Shoot, he told me that to keep me from running around at night and going to those suppers. But I got me a butcher knife and put it in my belt and went on to the supper. And I never did meet that bear and that bear better be glad I didn't.[33]

The St. Louis piano player and guitarist Henry Townsend also knew and worked with Johnson. Like Shines, he scoffed at the Johnson legend: "I heard at the end of the rainbow there's a pot of gold. But, see, I was smart enough even when I was a kid. We were living in the city, and I was a sufficient scientist and I would make me a little mist of rain and you could see a little rainbow in there. And I knew there wasn't any pot of gold right there in the yard. So I believe in selling your soul to the devil the same way I believe in the pot of gold at the end of the rainbow."[34]

Musicians such as Townsend and Shines are the ultimate debunkers.

They knew Johnson, worked with him, and traveled with him. If Johnson actively encouraged people to believe he was in a pact or relationship with the devil, as some of the biographies contend, wouldn't Townsend or Shines have heard him say something to that effect? "No, he never told me that lie, no," Shines once told an interviewer. "If he would have, I'd have called him a liar right to his face, because I know it's a lie."[35]

Let's keep in mind that the crossroads legend was initially applied to Robert Johnson not because he himself believed it or because other musicians whispered about it behind his back but mainly because he supposedly learned a lot of music in a short time. Even though the quick-learner story has long since been exposed as a fraud—or, in the less malignant construction, a fetching tall tale—the Faustian legend it spawned continues to stand with no visible means of support.

It should now be clear that after all the tedious fly-specking of the song texts, all the interviews, and all the thousands of words that have been written and spoken on the subject, there is no verifiable link between Robert Johnson and the devil. The historical evidence is tainted by hearsay, dubious research, compromised methodology, and questionable reporting. Even the folkloric evidence is too threadbare to stand up under close scrutiny. Most significantly of all, a majority of the musicians who were close to Johnson are on record as saying the story is a crock.

Even at this late date, new evidence and more credible testimony may yet come to light. But the existing paper trail, we contend, shows that the hallowed Johnson legend was constructed well after Johnson's lifetime to support a romanticized image of an American musical icon and make Johnson more appealing to people who were unfamiliar with his culture. Notwithstanding the commercial implications of a little romance, the effort was wasted. Johnson was more than talented enough to stand on his own merits, without the buttressing of fiction.

On that note, let us attempt a fresh consideration of Robert Johnson— a consideration based not on tall tales but on what we know concerning who he really was (admittedly a difficult target to hit from a distance of more than sixty years), how he lived, and what he really sang about.

13   Who Was He, Really?

He was pure legend.
> —Martin Scorsese, quoted in Alan Greenberg, *Love in Vain*

He was a nice boy, just crazy about women.
> —Son House, quoted in Stephen Calt and Gayle Dean
> Wardlow, "Robert Johnson"

He was the cutest little brown thing you've ever seen in your life.
> —Willie Mae Powell, quoted in *The Search for Robert Johnson*

In considering the blues of Robert Johnson, searching for hidden meanings makes for a diverting intellectual exercise, as we have seen. But it's easy to get carried away, because blues-idiom poetry is fluid enough to accommodate multiple interpretations. And as we have seen, interpretation is often influenced more by what the reader brings to the reading than by what's there in the lyrics. As an extreme example, imagine how a urologist might interpret "Stones in My Passway." The diagnosis would have to be kidney stones, so severe as to bring on pains in Johnson's heart, loss of appetite and libido, and acute embarrassment over his condition.

The point is that context isn't merely important; it is decisive in arriving at a rational interpretation of Johnson's songs. And even if one is unable or unwilling to read Robert Johnson's songs in the broader context of rural African American culture during the twenties and thirties, or of other blues by other artists from Johnson's era, each song can at least be read in the context of Johnson's other known songs. After all, only twenty-nine were ever recorded. So let's give it a try.

Taken in the context of Johnson's usual subjects, "Stones in My Passway" was not a urinary lament. It was another seduction song describing the differences between kind and unkind women. A kindhearted woman opened her door and let Johnson in, as he begged his woman to do in this song. An unkind woman—as described in this and other Johnson songs—entertained bad thoughts, studied evil, cheated on him, mistreated him, and tried to take his life and all his loving, too. His response to the unkind was ambivalence: "I got a woman that I'm loving, boy, but she don't mean a thing," so he had no qualms about leaving, or as he phrased it in the final verse, "I'm booked and I got to go."

In take 1 of "Rambling on My Mind" Johnson sang, "I got mean things all on my mind." Why? Because of mistreatment by his woman: "you treats me so unkind." In take 2 he took a little different tack, telling us that his woman had "devilment on her mind." Here again, keeping the song in context, it wasn't satanism but unfaithfulness, mischief, or disobedience that troubled him—again because his woman treated him "so unkind."

The rhyme between *unkind* and *mind* in "Rambling" takes us back to the *time-mind* rhyme in the first song Johnson ever recorded, "Kindhearted Woman Blues," in which his supposedly kindhearted sweetie studied evil all the time. In response Johnson told her, "You just as well to kill me as to have it on your mind"—meaning roughly that the thought is parent to the deed or, in this case, warning her not even to think about cheating or mistreating him. The song contrasted kindhearted women who did for him and evil-hearted women who did to him. He loved this woman; she didn't love him. Sometimes he eased his suspicions with drink, and other times he threatened his woman directly, warning that someday he would shake her hand good-bye and give her no more loving because he just wasn't satisfied.

Although Johnson sang of beating a girlfriend and having "mean things" on his mind, he was more often the victim of mean things in his real-life relationships. "He had a temper," recalled Johnny Shines, "but he never got the best of it. Lot of people punch him down. . . . like he'd get himself all beat up all the time."[1] Shines recalled a married woman named Louise who traveled with Johnson for a time. Louise could drink, sing, and dance and even played a little guitar. As Shines saw it, she was perfect for Johnson, but then Louise and Robert got into an argument late one night: "And he's standing up by one of these big old potbellied stoves with the eye up in the middle of it at the top. He started playing with the stove eye, telling Louise what he's going to do to her. And she got up and went over in the corner. She walked over to where he was, reached and got the stove eye. Bang! She laid him out with it. And I laughed. What you laughing about? This broad has knocked this man's brains out with a foolish ass stove eye. 'I'm not playing.'"[2]

Willie Coffee, one of Johnson's childhood chums, recalled a woman chasing Johnson down a road and threatening him with an ice pick. He kept leaping from one side to the other of a roadside drainage ditch, Coffee said, while the would-be assailant used a bridge to cross over and back. Finally Johnson was able to hitch a ride back to his mother's house, so he eluded the pick-wielding woman. "She swore she was going to kill him," Coffee said. Later, he recalled, that same woman "got killed at the jook house."[3]

In "Me and the Devil Blues" Johnson sang, "I'm going to beat my woman until I get satisfied." Yet there is scant evidence that the lyric was a reflection of the way he treated women. Only one of Johnson's girlfriends, Queen Elizabeth, is on record as saying he hit her. It happened just once, she said, and she would have killed him right on the spot if she had been able to get her hands on a shotgun.

These incidents help explain why some musicians were leery of traveling with Johnson. It was easy enough to get beat up, stabbed, or shot in a jook joint; why ask for trouble by making aggressive passes at the women in the place, as Johnson typically did? David "Honeyboy" Edwards said women would sometimes try to buy drinks for him or sit nearby and talk to him when he was performing, but he resolved early in his career to steer clear of any woman who was at a jook joint with her boyfriend or husband. "At that time, he'd kill you about her, 'cause he don't want to lose that woman," Edwards recalled. "You know he got a nice little woman and he feels, 'I won't get nothing like this no more.' He'd kill you about her. It's true. It really is. I used to sit down at night, lay down, and think about these things and map it out. And I say, 'That's true—leave those women alone if you want to live.'"⁴

The blues legend Son House recalled telling Johnson, "You have to be careful 'cause you mighty crazy about the girls. When you playing for these balls and these girls get full of that corn whiskey and snuff mixed together, and you be playing a good piece and they like it and come up and call you 'Daddy, play it again, daddy,' well don't let it run you crazy. You liable to get killed."⁵ But Johnson was undeterred. And despite the danger implicit in his flirtations, not to mention the times he got himself "all beat up," Johnson was, by all accounts, enormously successful at charming women—charming many, recalled Shines, but sustaining close or long-term relationships with only two or three: Louise, the married woman who traveled with him for a time; Estella Coleman, Robert Lockwood's mother; and the sister of the harmonica wizard Big Walter Horton. In letters to Pete Welding, Shines asked: "Did Robert really love? Yes, like a hobo loves a train . . . off one and on the other. . . . No woman really had an iron hand on Robert at any time. When his time came to go, he just went. . . . Heaven help him, he was not discriminating . . . probably a bit like Christ: He loved them all . . . the old, young, thin, fat and the short. They were all alike to Robert."⁶

This view of Johnson was consistent among contemporaries—friends as well as fellow musicians—who had opportunities to see him interact with women. He came on to all of them, without fear or favor, and music was a potent charm in his mojo bag of pickup techniques. Other musicians said he routinely sang his songs directly to women in his audience, hoping to get an offer of food, shelter, and maybe a little money. He addressed his songs to women in jooks, on the street, or anywhere else he happened to be playing. It is no surprise, then, that he addressed women in all but two of his recorded songs, the two exceptions being "They're Red Hot," a hokum piece, and "Preaching Blues," in which he addressed the blues personified.

The other twenty-seven songs were addressed to women. Johnson called them by name (or by double-entendre metaphor), offered them advice, pleaded with them, gave them instructions, begged them for help, and threatened to leave them, but most often he asked them questions.

This interactive, dialogue-like quality is common in all blues but was a dominant feature in Johnson's.

There is only one possible conclusion: If Johnson's songs contain clues to anything in his life—and that's all we're talking about here, clues—it is not that he was a tormented man, or a loner, or a satanist, or a closet believer in sorcery. It is that he was a notorious womanizer. Across the board, his contemporaries described him as such. So why have the songs been invested with so many dark and mysterious meanings? Why is Johnson regarded differently from all other blues artists? Why is Robert Johnson alone portrayed as a depression-era Faust who gave up his soul, sanity, and salvation in a crossroads exchange for musical genius?

The answers may lie, at least in part, in one generation's need to explain how and why it was sent into raptures by the words and music of an obscure Mississippi bluesman who had been dead for over twenty years. We refer to the generation of middle-class kids, mainly white, who grew up in the fifties and sixties—a generation that listened to African American music (R&B mostly) but was largely clueless when it came to African American culture, history, or vernacular. Thanks to Columbia's first reissue album, many of those middle-class baby boomers lost their blues virginity to Robert Johnson,[7] and it was an experience they never forgot. You can almost sense the reverential posture in this recollection from author Russell Banks: "I don't know if it's still true of listeners today, but blues fans of my age like to tell about the first time they heard Robert Johnson. It resembles our compulsion to say where we were when Kennedy was killed and our lives were unexpected filled with American history (or so it seemed then), and we needed to say how it felt. When we first listened to Robert Johnson, it was the long, sharp blade of American musical history that we felt pass through us, and it, too, scared us."[8] This parallels the recollections of such writers as Peter Guralnick, Pete Welding, Greil Marcus, Robert Palmer, and others—sixties veterans who were seduced by Johnson's music, who found the experience scary, shattering, chilling, or breathtaking, and who needed to confess how their lives were changed or affected by that first encounter.

The "discovery" of Robert Johnson and other traditional blues artists by large numbers of middle-class Americans occurred, as briefly noted in chapter 5, in the context of an unusual shift in pop-culture musical tastes.

By the end of the fifties, rock and roll had largely lost touch with its R&B, country and western, and gospel roots, and much of the music on the pop charts fell into the novelty or "Teen Angel" categories, aimed mainly at very young adolescents.[9] The "invasion" of British bands that would breathe new life into rock was still several years away, and as the popularity of rock waned among adults and older teens, the popularity of old-time music began to climb. Mockingly dubbed the "Dreaded Folk Revival" by a few veteran performers of old-time music, the brief ascendancy of folk forms between 1958 and 1965 spawned countless popularized imitations of traditional music, some of which were hugely successful.[10] The revival also spawned a broader awareness of what were considered "authentic" folk performers, including the African American blues artists whose recordings from the twenties and thirties offered glimpses of a little-understood niche in American culture and society. The old blues recordings, originally issued as 78-rpm shellac records and once prized for their rarity, started to become more widely available as collections held by recording companies, private individuals, and the Library of Congress were transcribed and reissued on long-play vinyl, effectively democratizing what had once been the exclusive sphere of serious jazz collectors. Some of the artists who made those early records—Sleepy John Estes, Yank Rachell, Son House, Mississippi John Hurt, Skip James, and Bukka White among them—were discovered to be still alive, and even if their chops weren't what they used to be, these blues elders nonetheless became late-life headliners at campus concerts, nightclubs, and festivals.

In striving to understand why, of all the old blues artists, Johnson was singled out for special veneration by the sixties generation, it may be important to remember that Johnson already had been lionized in the jazz criticism of an earlier generation. And three jazz writers associated with that generation, Samuel B. Charters, John H. Hammond Jr., and Frank Driggs, figured prominently in presenting Johnson to the young Americans who were caught up in the revival of old-time music. In 1959 Charters included "Preaching Blues," arguably the most technically dazzling of Johnson's recordings, on the LP that accompanied *The Country Blues,* the influential book in which Charters extolled Johnson's artistry as "consistently brilliant" and said that some of Johnson songs were suggestive of inner "torment." In 1961 Hammond, who had returned to Columbia

Records as executive producer in 1959 after an absence of thirteen years, released the first full album of Johnson reissues (recorded from the original Vocalion masters, no less). And Driggs, the album's producer, authored the memorable liner notes that cast Johnson as a shy, mysterious folk genius—tormented, too, of course—who recorded wonderful music and then disappeared. The portrayal of Johnson as a folk artist no doubt made a powerful impression on young members of the sixties counterculture, many of whom were already smitten with the popular image of folk singers as loners whose art expressed a weightier view of the human condition.

To both generations—the early jazz buffs and the counterculture "folkies"—Johnson's very obscurity may have added to his appeal. It certainly added to his malleability in the hands of those who sought to understand him. He was an impressively talented African American musician who had died young and who could now be invested with whatever cultural, psychological, and biographical baggage his impressionable fans might divine from his singing, his lyrics, or the lyrical inventions of the former jazz writers. The inventions, as we have seen, were plentiful. The young fans who were swept up in the mythology and mystique that quickly filled the information vacuum around Johnson included a number of the future researchers and folklorists who would later turn blues scholarship into a true discipline and help interpret Johnson for succeeding generations. The sixties-era fans also included such future rock stars as Keith Richards and Eric Clapton. They, too, would emerge later to help lionize Johnson for the legions of fans in the seventies and eighties to whom the artist was marketed as a father of rock and roll. The British stars unabashedly celebrated Johnson as the most important blues musician in history and likened his guitar playing to the music of Bach. Clapton proclaimed his singing "the most powerful cry" extant in the human voice.[11]

An arresting voice, virtuoso guitar playing, indecipherable words, suggestions of psychic anguish, death at an early age, the touching anecdotes promulgated as part of the initial liner-note mythology—it all seemed to support the Faustian tragedy that was eventually constructed to explain Johnson's art. Even if the mythology was not embraced as literal fact by baby boomers, it became a shared frame of reference, distinguishing those who had been touched by Johnson from those who had not and, in later years, knowledgeable old hands from the uninformed newcomers who discovered Johnson through *The Complete Recordings* in 1991. As we have seen, however, many of the knowledgeable old hands embraced the mythology as literal fact. Not only that, but they employed their considerable skills as critics, researchers, and scholarly writers to reconstruct Johnson as the protagonist in a neoclassical tragedy about the unbearable burden of great talent.

The point that must be made is this: Robert Johnson's life was tragic, but only because it ended so early. There is no morality play here. Johnson lived the life he did—singing songs, drinking, and begging favors from every woman he met—not because he was haunted by apocalyptic or supernatural images but because it was the life he chose to live.

Despite the pain that undoubtedly was caused by the loss of his first wife and their child, there is no evidence that his grief (or the alleged censure of his wife's family) caused Johnson to embrace Satan. One contemporary recalled that Johnson would occasionally curse God when drunk, but no one who spent time with him in the years following the loss could recall him saying or doing anything to promote the idea that he was in an ongoing partnership with the devil. One of the documentary films on Johnson suggested that he might have turned to music after the loss to escape his grief.[12] But we know that Johnson was already trying to become a professional musician before his wife's death. A more mundane reading, consistent with what we know about other blues musicians who lost their spouses, is that Virginia's death left Robert free to pursue his overriding ambition and become a walking musician.

The persistent image of Johnson as a driven outsider pursued by the hounds of hell dates back to Rudi Blesh's 1946 essay. But Johnson's need to keep moving had less to do with hellhounds than with Greyhounds. He rode Greyhound buses and passenger trains, hitched rides, hopped freights, and kept walking because there was no such thing as a long-term, big-money engagement for an African American street performer in the middle of the Great Depression. He had to keep moving from place to place to make money.

When he performed on street corners, he could draw on a vast repertoire of songs that branched into virtually every niche of American music, but his twenty-nine recorded songs were blues. Those songs give powerful testimony to Johnson's skill as an artist and showman, but all twenty-nine are well within blues tradition. As an instrumentalist Johnson developed nuances of style that were considered innovative and exciting by his contemporaries, but he remained solidly in touch with the oral tradition of the rural South, a tradition in which musicians created their own spontaneous arrangements by attending to each other's chord changes, techniques, and vocal shadings. Henry Townsend said Johnson totally "outmanned" him as a guitarist, but it didn't matter when they worked together. "He was one of the people if you played it right, he could play with you," Townsend said. "If you played it wrong, he could play with you. And whatever you do it was right for him because he was just that bright."[13]

Despite the rumors concerning the black arts, there was nothing portentous or supernatural about Johnson's death. He took up with a woman, as he did in almost every place he went, and he supposedly was poisoned by the woman's jealous husband—a murder attempt that left him too weak to fight off the infection that may have been the immediate cause of his death. Given his occupation and the violent venues in which he played his music, Johnson's death wasn't even all that unusual. Nor was his life. He wanted to be an artist, not a farmer, so he lived the artist's life as best he could given the social and economic conditions of his time. He faced the same challenges and choices faced by dozens, perhaps hundreds, of itinerant musicians who lived and often died in similar circumstances, victims of alcohol, envy, jook-house violence, disease, or the perils of the road.

Musicians who knew Johnson testified that he was a nice guy and fairly average—except, of course, for his musical talent, his weakness for whiskey and women, and his commitment to the road. He drank because it was the medium of exchange in the venues he worked or because drink gave him strength or nerve. He was forward with women and treated them in a predatory manner because he and other bluesmen relied on women for meals and beds. In sum, he was a typical walking musician who stuck to the road and hung out with other musicians until the end of his life.

Peter Guralnick, for one, has argued that the soul-selling legend is the highest tribute that could possibly be paid to Johnson, the ultimate attempt to explain a great artist's talent.[14] Given that argument, one would expect to find other artists about whom similar legends have been constructed. Yet, once again, Johnson stands virtually alone.[15] In our view, the stories that have been concocted about Johnson represent an abuse of legend—that is, they do nothing to help us understand the man or his art. As long as he is mythologized as a shy loner, tormented genius, nihilist, or satanist, he loses his ties to the community whose art he represents. Critics, fans, and casual listeners can keep him at a safe distance, becoming intimate with his music on *their* terms, not his, and commercial promoters can endlessly appropriate, revamp, and repackage his image for successive groups of music consumers. All this is harmless enough, one supposes, except that it offends the memories of people, such as Robert "Junior" Lockwood, who had an opportunity to see Robert Johnson as he really was: "There are some people who want to try to get some glory because Robert is so popular. They say they knew Robert, and they don't know a damn thing. They talked about him selling his soul to the devil. I want to know how you do that. If anybody sold their souls to the devil, it's the groups that have to have a million dollars worth of dope and have a million dollars in money to play. I don't like the way they are trying to label him. He was a blues musician. Just like the rest of them."[16]

Well, maybe not exactly like the rest of them. But he was enough like them to deserve consideration not as a mythic figure but as an artist who has something to tell us about the vitality and resiliency of African American culture in the rural South.

Robert Johnson, Honeyboy Edwards, Johnny Shines, Son House, Sunnyland Slim, Henry Townsend, Bukka White, Sonny Boy Williamson no. 2—with artists such as these, there is simply no need to dramatize their lives with invented stories, for their lives were more than dramatic enough. In 1928, for example, House pulled a gun and shot a man to death at a house party near Clarksdale, Mississippi; he spent two years in jail before his claim of self-defense was given due consideration. Townsend ambushed the bluesman J. D. "Jelly Jaw" Short, shooting the man in the groin to avenge what Townsend claimed was Short's attempt on his life. White served time in the Delta's notorious Parchman Farm prison after wounding a man during a fight in Aberdeen, Mississippi. Williamson, who often carried a pistol (and fired it in anger on at least one occasion), once became so enraged when his band showed up late for a gig that he fired the whole group and played the engagement as a solo. Memphis Minnie, one of the most popular artists of her era, survived in the violent world of Delta blues by becoming "tougher than a man"—a tobacco-chewing brawler who would fight with fists, knives, or whatever was available. As a matter of fact, most of these artists probably would have preferred a little less drama, a little less violence, and a little more security. They faced life-threatening dangers every day in order to be, as Johnny Shines phrased it, under no one's command. They created art under extreme conditions, and in the process, they provided good times when times were hard.

As a participant in a remarkable chapter of American history, and as an inhabitant of a sometimes savage underworld of jooks, jails, and Jim Crow, Robert Johnson endured hardships and took chances—perhaps even foolish chances—so that he could exercise agency over his own life. He also found the time to leave a recorded musical legacy, one that continues to enrich our lives. And just as Johnson's music stands on its own, with no need of embellishment, so does his life. He more than earned the right to have his likeness on a postage stamp and to be venerated as one of the twentieth century's most potent voices.

But he was still a man—and a walking blues musician. Very much like the rest of them.

Notes

Chapter 2: Our Hero

1. Although most researchers now accept this date, the evidence is not conclusive. Mississippi did not begin keeping birth records until 1912. School records, marriage licenses, and Johnson's 1938 death certificate suggest birth years of 1908, 1909, 1910, and 1912. Because Johnson was not listed on census tracts for 1910, however, the 1908 and 1909 dates are the least persuasive. See Freeland, "He Would Go Out," 49.

2. Calt and Wardlow, "Robert Johnson," 41–50.

3. For more information on Johnson during his time in the Hazlehurst area, see Freeland, "He Would Go Out."

4. Standard dictionaries still give "*juke* as the correct spelling, but the blues musician Howard "Louie Bluie" Armstrong, a National Heritage Award recipient, insists that it was always spelled *jook* in the African American community. Other experts say *jook,* used as both a noun and a verb, most likely evolved from similar-sounding West African words meaning "infamous" or "disorderly." Jook joints predated the invention of coin-operated jukeboxes.

5. Wardlow interview, 2002.

6. *Walking musician* was the term many Delta artists used to describe themselves and their itinerant existence. The bluesman Big Joe Williams, who taught David "Honeyboy" Edwards to play guitar, said this of his protégé: "He was a walking musician, just like myself, all down through that Delta and through the hills—Vicksburg, Leland, Clarksdale, all over there" (Williams interview, 1969). His fellow Delta bluesman Joe Willie Wilkins called himself "the walking Seeburg," referring to a jukebox brand name. Edwards summed up the musician's existence this way: "If I couldn't make a quarter in a city, I was gone" (see Pearson, *Sounds So Good,* 21, 147).

7. Stephen Calt, one of Johnson's biographers, finds evidence that it was Speir who went looking for Johnson somewhere in Louisiana. This is plausible given Speir's interest in the commer-

cial potential of African American music. But it seems unlikely that Speir would have taken such a trip in the midthirties, since by most accounts, including his own, he had grown disenchanted with the recording business by that time.

8. Although recent research suggests that the studio of radio station KONO, located in the Blue Bonnet Hotel, was the site of Johnson's initial sessions, most sources claim the recording was done in a makeshift studio in San Antonio's Gunter Hotel. See James, "Robert Johnson," 26–27.

9. *A&R* used to be a common recording industry shorthand for artist and repertory supervisors, whose responsibility generally was to help artists convey their work in ways that would be both representative and commercially appealing. The current term is *producer.*

10. Pearson, *Sounds So Good,* 15–17.

11. Based largely on the recollection of Honeyboy Edwards, early researchers tried to find a store with the name Three Forks, ultimately finding one at Quito, some thirteen miles southwest of Greenwood. For years that store was thought to be the place where Johnson played his last two gigs. Later, however, Edwards insisted that the bluesman was hired to play at a jook behind a store at the intersection of U.S. 49E and U.S. 82, barely three miles east of Greenwood. That store, then known as Shaeffer's, is now believed by researchers to have been the scene of Johnson's final job. The store is no longer there, having been destroyed by a storm in the early forties. (The building that once housed Three Forks is also gone; it was razed circa 2001.)

12. Edwards, in a 1978 interview with Pearson (*Sounds So Good,* 16), indicated that the woman could walk to town to see Johnson because the distance was only "about two and a half miles," a recollection that tends to support the belief that Johnson played his final gigs at the jook behind Shaeffer's.

13. Although there have been various suppositions, assumptions, and accusations about who poisoned the whiskey, the guitar player Ce Dell Davis, who was still a child in 1938, recalled many years later that he heard it was a woman known as Craphouse Bea who carried the doctored bottle to Johnson. See Pearson, "Ce Dell Davis' Story," 10.

14. This is the essence of the account Honeyboy Edwards gave to interviewers in the sixties and seventies. Later, his memory refreshed by the discovery of a death certificate showing that Johnson died on Tuesday, August 16, Edwards recalled visiting the artist on Monday, August 15.

15. Alan Greenberg, the author of a screenplay about Johnson, says this information came from Mack McCormick. In Greenberg's screenplay, which draws from the legend that Johnson bartered his soul to the devil, Tush Hog is the devil, or devilman. Despite any supernatural implications, Tush Hog is a common nickname in Alabama and Mississippi, where it identifies a tough guy or fighter.

16. Two other Johnson grave markers exist in the Greenwood area. In 1990 *Living Blues* magazine published testimony from a one-time Johnson girlfriend

identifying the Payne Chapel M. B. Church in the hamlet of Quito, southwest of Greenwood, as the place where the bluesman was buried. A rock band later placed a small marker at that site. Johnson's death certificate, however, stated that he was buried at "Zion Church," and the search for that site led to Mount Zion M. B. Church, three or four miles south of Quito. In 1991 a large monument was placed at the Mount Zion location by Columbia Records. In the year 2000 LaVere located a woman named Rose Eskridge who had been living on Star of the West Plantation in 1938 and who recalled that her late husband, Tom, had been hired to dig a grave at Little Zion M. B. Church for a traveling musician who had died on the plantation. That testimony, coupled with the nearness of the residence where Johnson was believed to have died, pointed strongly to Little Zion Church as the correct burial site.

Chapter 3: The Anecdotes

1. Country Music Hall of Fame, *Encyclopedia of Country Music,* 290–91. Regarding Brunswick/ARC's approach to the San Antonio sessions, the *San Antonio Light* newspaper reported: "Brunswick recording crew here figures it set a record when it got under the wire with 105 recordings made in the first three days of its San Antonio set up." See Obrecht, "Robert Johnson," 8.

2. Charters, *Robert Johnson,* 15.

3. Ibid., 16.

4. Shines interview, 1991.

5. Ibid.

6. Although legend confidently places these events on November 22, the night before the first recording session, evidence strongly suggests that the run-in with police occurred after the first session and thus may have been responsible for the two-day gap between session 1 and session 2. Steve James notes that Don Law himself recalled the difficulty he had securing Johnson's release from jail for a session on Thanksgiving, which fell on November 26 that year. See James, "Robert Johnson," 26–27.

7. Excerpt, *Can't You Hear the Wind Howl?* (film).

8. Hammond, "Jim Crow Blues," 27–28.

9. Hammond was connected to at least one other spurious blues legend. After Bessie Smith was fatally injured in an automobile accident near Clarksdale, Mississippi, in late 1937, several jazz musicians told Hammond that the singer died because she had been denied admission to a whites-only hospital. Hammond, a lifelong civil-rights advocate, passed the story along through his network of friendly journalists and music-business executives, and for decades afterward the story was accepted as fact, even though it was apocryphal.

10. The reference to black arts first appeared in a quotation attributed to Shines in a 1966 essay about Johnson; see Welding, "Hell Hound," 73–76.

11. Hammond, liner notes, *Spirituals to Swing,* 1959.

12. Charters, *Country Blues,* 208.

13. As reported by Bob Groom in a two-page biography of Johnson in a British magazine; see Groom, "Robert Johnson," 10–11. While the details of this hearsay account are unclear, it is interesting to note the implied place of death (Friars Point), the instrument of foul play (a knife), and the suggested motive (retaliation following a slap).

14. Berendt's book was first published, in German, in 1953 and was revised in 1958 and 1968. The 1975 English-language version, which constituted the third major revision, showed Berendt to be decidedly liberal in his blues tastes. He praised Captain Beefheart and proclaimed, "There are more blues movements and blues styles today than ever before and they all live side by side." We do not know which revision of the book introduced the misinformation about Johnson's death; the misinformation is similar to that reported by Charters in 1959.

15. Hammond with Townsend, *John Hammond on Record,* 202.

16. Pearson, *Sounds So Good,* 17.

17. Napier and Williamson, "I Knew Robert Johnson," 96.

18. Stephen C. LaVere endorsed the latter version, saying Johnson was able to survive a dose of strychnine but contracted fatal pneumonia in the process. See LaVere, liner notes, *Complete Recordings,* 18. Luther Wade, the white owner of the property where Johnson died, was the informant for the notation, on the back of the death certificate, that Johnson had died of complications of syphilis.

Chapter 4: Early Notices

1. Although most left-wing causes and organizations have long since been marginalized in this country, they commanded relatively more interest and attention in the thirties. Many well-meaning Americans saw in socialism the seeds of a more humane, even utopian, alternative to the economic misery brought by the Great Depression.

2. Johnson, "Sight and Sound," 29.

3. Hammond, "Sight and Sound," 30; in all previously published research on Johnson, this passage has been attributed to a British music publication called *Melody Maker.* Most sources agree the item was published by *Melody Maker* in July 1937, which, if correct, would be one month after the publication in *New Masses.* Hammond contributed to both publications.

4. A staunch supporter of equal opportunity for African Americans long before the cause became politically acceptable in the United States, Hammond joined the board of the National Association for the Advancement of Colored People in 1937 and later served as NAACP vice president.

5. Smith, *Jazz Record Book,* 259.

6. Just where this idea came from remains an enigma. One might logically guess that the authors were referring to Lonnie Johnson, even though he

qualified as an old-time New Orleans guitar player only by virtue of having been born there in 1894; his playing became more closely associated with St. Louis and Chicago. It's clear that Robert Johnson respected and emulated Lonnie, so much so that according to biographer Stephen C. LaVere, the younger musician sometimes claimed his middle initial stood for Lonnie rather than Leroy. It's also possible the two might have met in St. Louis. Such speculation aside, one wonders whether the authors jumped to a conclusion about Robert's musical training after listening to his later recordings, which showed his debt to Lonnie, or worked from the belief, then common among jazz buffs, that New Orleans was a primal source of jazz. Whatever, the reference was (and still is) uninformative, adding mystery rather than clarification.

7. Blesh, *Shining Trumpets,* 121–22. Blesh apprently tried to display his familiarity with ethnic slang when he used *easy rider* to describe a guitar. In fact, the term usually referred to a sexual partner.

8. Guralnick, "Searching," 27.

9. Blesh, *Shining Trumpets,* 110.

10. Ibid., 3.

11. Hammond with Townsend, *John Hammond on Record,* 202, 206.

12. Charters, *Country Blues,* 210.

13. Ibid., 208.

14. Welding, "The Robert Johnson I Knew," 18, 32.

15. The British rocker Keith Richards, a charter member of the Rolling Stones band, recalled that when he heard one of Johnson's recordings for the first time, he asked, "Who's the other guy playing with him?" Realizing that Johnson was playing the complex figures by himself, and doing it while singing, Richards said he concluded that Johnson "must have three brains." (These comments come from an interview, excerpts from which can be found in the liner notes to the CD set *Robert Johnson: The Complete Recordings* and in the Victor Bockris biography of Richards.)

16. Shines interview, 1991.

17. O'Brien, "Dark Road" (pt. 1 [1983]), 9.

18. Welding, "The Robert Johnson I Knew," 18, 32.

Chapter 5: The Reissue Project, Phase One

1. This is one of several colorful descriptions of Johnson's relationships with women found in letters that Shines wrote to the jazz critic Pete Welding. See Shines, "The Robert Johnson I Knew," 30–33.

2. Welding, "Hell Hound," 73–76.

3. Ibid., 73.

4. Oliver, *Conversations,* 188.

5. Oliver, *Story of the Blues,* 119.

6. Although some fellow musicians mentioned Johnson's bad eye, photographs show him to have been a handsome man, just as his ex-girlfriends and

other contemporaries attested. Musicians who traveled with Johnson described him as assertive, but not violent, with women.

Chapter 6: Reissue, Phase Two

1. Waxman, liner notes, *King of the Delta Blues Singers;* Waxman later went on to get a law degree and is now an attorney, executive producer, and talent manager based in New York.

2. Generally speaking, sixties-era British rock groups were more consciously in touch with blues than were their American counterparts. The Rolling Stones took their name from an early Muddy Waters recording. The Yardbirds and the Animals covered songs by Billy Boy Arnold, Eddie Boyd, John Lee Hooker, and Jimmy Reed and were among the British groups eager to back such American blues artists as Sonny Boy Williamson no. 2 during European tours. When the Beatles began their first U.S. tour in 1965, they were asked by a member of the press what they hoped to see during their visit. Muddy Waters, came the reply. "Where's that?" the reporter supposedly asked.

3. Welding, liner notes to *King of the Delta Blues Singers.*

4. Shines made comments to this effect in a number of interviews. The comments paraphrased here are heard in the 1997 documentary film *Can't You Hear the Wind Howl?*

5. Welding, "The Robert Johnson I Knew," 18, 32.

6. Ferris, "Robert Johnson," 28.

7. Guralnick, *Feel Like Going Home,* 36.

8. Cook, *Listen to the Blues,* 74.

9. Charters, *Robert Johnson,* 22.

10. The Charters count also could be considered unreliable on the grounds that Charters himself professed to find Johnson's words "almost impossible to understand."

11. After Johnson ran away, House said, "He stayed, looked like to me, about six months. Willie and I were playing again out at a little place east of Robinsonville called Banks, Mississippi. We were playing there one Saturday night and, all of a sudden, somebody came in through the door. Who but him! He had a guitar swinging on his back. I said, 'Bill!' He said, 'Huh?' I said 'Look who's coming in the door.' He looked and said, 'Yeah, Little Robert.' I said, 'And he's got a guitar.' And Willie and I laughed about it. Robert finally wiggled through the crowd and got to where we were. He spoke, and I said, 'Well, boy, you still got a guitar, huh? What do you do with that thing? You can't do nothing with it.' He said, 'Well, I'll tell you what.' I said, 'What?' He said, 'Let me have your seat a minute.' So I said, 'All right, and you better do something with it, too.' And I winked my eye at Willie. So he sat down there and finally got started. And man! He was so good! When he finished all our mouths were standing open. I said, 'Well, ain't that fast! He's gone now!'" (see Charters, *Robert Johnson,* 7–8). Although Charters did not say where this story

came from, the account follows, word for word, a portion of Julius Lester's lengthy interview of Son House, originally published as Son House, "I Can Make My Own Songs."

12. Charters, *Robert Johnson,* 9.

13. Ibid., 22.

14. Evans interview, 1993.

15. Marcus, *Mystery Train,* 22–23, 24, 30.

16. Ibid., 29.

17. Oakley, *The Devil's Music,* 199.

18. *The Search for Robert Johnson* (film), Willie Mae Powell interview fragment.

19. *Can't You Hear the Wind Howl?* (film), Willie Mason interview fragment.

20. Welding, "David 'Honey Boy' Edwards," 3–12.

21. Welding, "The Robert Johnson I Knew," 18, 32.

22. As far as we know, the original authority for this observation was Dick Waterman, the business manager and booking agent for a number of the old-time blues artists who launched second careers during the folk revival of the fifties and sixties. As quoted by Jim O'Neal in "I Once Was Lost" (376), Waterman's observation sounded almost like a warning to credulous researchers: "In talking to older bluesmen, you must be well aware that they are going to tell you what they think that you want to hear."

23. Pearson, *Sounds So Good,* 135–36.

24. Scherman, "The Hellhound's Trail," 41.

25. Neff and Connor, *Blues,* 56.

26. The St. Louis incident was described in one of two letters Shines sent to Pete Welding; see Shines, "The Robert Johnson I Knew," 32. The same story, told in the same words, appeared in Charters's book *Robert Johnson*

27. Palmer, *Deep Blues,* 126; Papa Legba is one of several names for a traditional West African deity, often described as a "trickster" god, who was associated with the crossroads and could grant certain kinds of favors.

28. *Hoodoo* is an African American term for magic—often, but not always, magic that inflicts bad luck or some other type of harm. In folk vernacular and among some scholars, the term is interchangeable with *voodoo,* although the latter is more appropriately applied to a neo-African religious system native to Haiti.

29. Finn, *The Bluesmen,* 212.

30. Ibid., 210.

Chapter 7: Myth Eclipses Reality

1. Iglauer and staff, "Reconstructing," 6–9.

2. McCormick supposedly was given one of the three photos by Johnson's sister before LaVere acquired rights to the remaining two, according to information on display at LaVere's blues museum in Greenwood, Mississippi.

3. N. A., "Forefathers," 48.
4. O'Brien, "Robert Johnson Photo," 9–10.
5. Barlow, *Looking Up at Down,* 49.
6. Kubik, *Africa and the Blues,* 22.
7. Ellison, *Extensions of the Blues,* 5.
8. Welding, "Muddy Waters: Gone to Main Street," 139.
9. *Can't You Hear the Wind Howl?* (film), interview excerpt.
10. Ibid.
11. Finn, *The Bluesmen,* 210.
12. Guralnick, "Searching," 40.

Chapter 8: Reissue, Phase Three

1. Miles, "Justice Hits the Charts," 1.
2. Brazier, "He Gone Straight to Hell," 10.
3. Lee, "This Fella Y'all Looking For," 2.
4. See *Musician* 147 (Jan. 1991).
5. Shea, "The Complete Recordings," n.p.
6. Charters, *The Blues Makers,* 219.
7. Ibid.
8. Powell is generally acknowledged to be the Willie Mae whom Johnson called by name in his song "Love in Vain."
9. The inteview was published in Leadbitter, ed., *Nothing but the Blues,* 132–40.
10. Like Edwards, Johnson's former traveling companion Johnny Shines spent considerable time on camera, offering recollections of his time with Johnson. Like Edwards, Shines was not asked about a satanic pact, nor was he asked about McCormick's assertion that Johnson was "drawn to that texture" of a partnership with Satan. Or if he was asked, the responses landed on the cutting-room floor.
11. Scherman, "The Hellhound's Trail," 46.
12. Lomax, *The Land Where the Blues Began,* 15.
13. In 1973 Samuel Charters wrote that some of the people who knew Johnson remembered his mother as Mary and his stepfather as Robert "Dusty" Johnson. Exactly who remembered those names Charters did not say. Most researchers later agreed that after the end of her marriage to Charles Dodds, a.k.a. Charles Spencer, Johnson's mother, Julia Major Dodds, married a sharecropper named Will Willis, whose nickname was Dusty.

Chapter 9: A Myth to the Twenty-first Century

1. Greenberg, *Love in Vain,* foreword.
2. Romanowski and George-Warren, eds., *New Rolling Stone Encyclopedia,* 517.

3. Tooze, *Muddy Waters*, 43.
4. Kubik, *Africa and the Blues*, xv.
5. George, *Hip Hop America*, 53.
6. Corsello, "John McEnroe," 56.
7. Bragg, "Mississippi Man Ruled Sole Heir," n.p.
8. Wheeler, "Are the Blues Fixin' to Die?" R3. The "crossroads" mentioned in this article is actually the intersection of U.S. 61 and U.S. 49, the Delta's principal highways. Steve Cheseborough, a scholar and musician who has researched Mississippi's blues sites, says it is implausible to suggest that any soul selling ever occurred anywhere in the Delta, much less at such a busy junction so close to a population center; see Cheseborough, *Blues Traveling*, 68–69.

Chapter 10: Satan and Sorcery

1. Wheatstraw marketed himself as the "High Sheriff from Hell" and the "Devil's Son-in-Law."
2. Evans, "Johnson, Robert Leroy," 650.
3. Evans, "Ramblin David Evans" (pt. 1), 12.
4. Evans, "Ramblin David Evans" (pt. 1), 12.
5. Ibid.
6. Calt, "Idioms of Robert Johnson," 56, 60.
7. Evans, "Ramblin David Evans" (pt. 1), 12.
8. Williamsinterview, 1969.
9. Calt, "Idioms of Robert Johnson," 59.
10. Evans, "Ramblin David Evans" (pt. 1) 13.

Chapter 11: The Song Texts

1. Lipsitz, *The Possessive Investment in Whiteness*, 126.
2. Shines interview, 1991.
3. Calt and Wardlow, "Robert Johnson," 44.
4. Strachwitz, phone conversation with Pearson, 1999.
5. See chapter 3, note 1.
6. LaVere, "Tying Up a Few Loose Ends," 33.
7. This is a common regional colloquialism connoting mischievous or unruly behavior.
8. Evans, "Ramblin David Evans" (pt. 1), 12.
9. Oliver, *Story of the Blues*, 119.
10. Another possible source could be W. Lee O'Daniel and his Hillbilly Boys, a group that recorded six masters the day before Johnson recorded.
11. Sam Charters came up with a similar interpretation of the song; see Charters, *Poetry of the Blues*, 109–10.
12. Shines interview, 1991.

13. Charters, *Poetry of the Blues,* 109.

14. Folk tradition includes references to supernatural encounters as taking place during the night and even in the morning, but the first choice for serious bargain hunters would be midnight.

15. Marcus, *Mystery Train,* 37.

16. Evans, liner notes, *Black Boy Shine,* 3.

17. Driggs, liner notes, *Robert Johnson.*

18. Evans, "Ramblin David Evans" (pt. 3), 12.

19. Oliver, *Blues Fell This Morning,* 278.

20. Oliver, *Story of the Blues,* 119.

21. The line is reminiscent of Papa Charlie Jackson's 1925 classic "Cats Got the Measles." In this tune Jackson sings about hearing a rumbling deep down in the ground, which, he says, "must have been the Devil chaining my good gal down." Jackson's verse is followed by the euphemistic blasphemy "Doggone my soul." Johnson may have been familiar with Jackson's earlier tune. Or Johnson's pairing of "dogging me around" and "spirit . . . deep down in the ground" may have been coincidental.

22. As in the ballad tradition, burial instructions in blues have their own set of conventions. In early blues one finds numerous verses that are aggressively sacrilegious, as in "When I die, don't bury daddy at all. . . . Just pickle my bones in alcohol" or "When I die just throw me in the sea. . . . So the tadpoles and minnows can made a fuss over me." By taking lightly what the church takes so seriously, the blues artists and audience challenge church authority in the manner suggested by Paul Oliver in *Blues Fell This Morning.*

23. Making things even more inbred, Temple was accompanied at that session by Charlie McCoy, Joe McCoy's brother.

24. Johnson also used weather imagery in a song of seduction when he told his woman, "You better come on in my kitchen, it's going to be raining outdoors."

25. LeRoux, "American Odyssey," 71.

26. This interesting sidelight to the story of Robert Johnson's recording sessions was unearthed by Chris Strachwitz of Arhoolie Records; see Law, "Letter," 7.

27. Blesh, *Shining Trumpets,* 121–22.

Chapter 12: A House of Cards

1. One could easily argue that overzealous readings of "Cross Road Blues" and "Hellhound on My Trail" were the actual source and that the quotation attributed to House was later seized as the long-sought confirmation of all the song-inspired speculation.

2. Wardlow, *Chasin' That Devil Music,* 203–4.

3. Welding, "Hell Hound on His Trail" (pt. 3 [1971]), 16.

4. Wardlow, *Chasin' That Devil Music,* 203.

5. Vernon interview, 2000.

6. Although the practice was not widespread, some early blues musicians strung their guitars in unorthodox ways, presumably to achieve distinctive sounds. Big Joe Williams, for one, created a nine-string guitar by doubling three of the six normal strings. Robert Johnson played a standard six-string guitar on his recordings and also posed with a six-string guitar in the only known photographs of him holding an instrument.

7. Welding, "Hell Hound" (pt. 3 [1971]), 16.

8. House, "I Can Make My Own," 42.

9. Edwards, *Crawling Kingsnake Blues* (sound recording).

10. Welding, "David 'Honeyboy' Edwards" (1971) 132–40.

11. Marcus, *Mystery Train,* 32.

12. Ibid., 24, 32.

13. Ibid., 32.

14. Russell, *The Blues,* 61.

15. E-mail response to an e-mail inquiry from McCulloch (2000) that specifically mentioned Welding's essay as a possible source. Russell said that any similarities to something Welding had published might have arisen because he (Russell) was "quoting someone quoting Welding, or because House said the same thing twice, or for any number of reasons." He added, "I do not have that Welding article on file."

16. Levet, "Stones in My Passway," 33.

17. Guralnick, "Searching," 30.

18. Wardlow, *Chasin' That Devil Music,* 107.

19. Evans interview, 1993.

20. Palmer, *Deep Blues,* 113.

21. Puckett, *Magic and Folk Beliefs,* 554.

22. Hyatt, *Hoodoo,* 97–111.

23. Conway, *African Banjo Echoes,* 78; the story cited by Conway was actually told by Trice to folklorist Bruce Bastin.

24. Welding, "Hell Hound" (pt. 3 [1971]), 17.

25. Shines interview, 1973; a similar quotation was given to Pearson during an interview in 1990.

26. Young, "Robert Johnson," 78.

27. O'Neal, "A Traveler's Guide," 24.

28. In 1991, for example, Edwards discussed the crossroads mythology in two workshop dialogues with Pearson at the Smithsonian Festival of American Folklife in Washington, D.C.

29. Edwards, *The World Don't Owe Me Nothing,* 105.

30. *Hellhounds on My Trail* (film), interview excerpt.

31. LaVere interview, 2002; at the time LaVere made this comment, his com-

pany's Web site, <http://www.deltahaze.com>, still included an animated red devil at the entry to the pages dealing with Johnson.

32. *The Search for Robert Johnson* (film), interview excerpt.

33. Shines interview, 1991.

34. Townsend interview, 1991.

35. *Can't You Hear the Wind Howl?* (film), interview excerpt.

Chapter 13: Who Was He, Really?

1. Shines interview, 1973.

2. Ibid.

3. *Hellhounds on My Trail* (film), interview excerpt.

4. Pearson, *Sounds So Good to Me*, 15.

5. House, "I Can Make My Own Songs," 42.

6. Shines, "The Robert Johnson I Knew," 32.

7. Most kids had already been exposed to urban blues artists, such as Chicago's Jimmy Reed, whose songs occasionally "crossed over" to hit the pop charts. Dancing to Reed's trademark guitar boogie at a high school social function was one thing, however, and understanding (or even being aware of) the rich tradition that underlay such music was quite another.

8. Banks, "The Devil and Robert Johnson," 27–31.

9. Even veteran jazz critic Rudi Blesh, who had welcomed the advent of rock and roll as a return to old-time barrelhouse blues, saw signs in the later fifties that rock and roll was losing its original fecundity. In a postscript to the 1958 revision of his book *Shining Trumpets: A History of Jazz,* Blesh voiced concern that rock and roll, which had introduced millions of jitterbugging teens to "primitive Negro music" (349), was being converted into just another "tin-pan alley concoction" (351).

10. The Kingston Trio's recording of "Tom Dooley," a ballad about Civil War veteran Tom Dula, who was hanged in North Carolina in 1868 after confessing to a murder that legend says may have been committed by a girlfriend, rose to number 1 on the pop charts in 1958. Also reaching number 1 on the charts in 1958 was Lloyd Price's "Stagger Lee," a high-energy, full-chorus version of the "Stack O'Lee Blues," an African American blues ballad dating back to the early nineteen hundreds. Peter, Paul, and Mary's recycling of Bob Dylan's "Blowin' in the Wind" got as high as number 2 in 1963.

11. Except from commentary in liner notes to *Robert Johnson: The Complete Recordings*.

12. *Can't You Hear the Wind Howl?* (film), excerpt of narrator Danny Glover.

13. Townsend interview, 1991.

14. *Hellhounds on My Trail* (film), excerpt of Guralnick's presentation at Rock and Roll Hall of Fame and Museum.

15. Some sources implicate violinist Niccolò Paganini in a devil deal and suggest that Paganini himself encouraged others to believe the story. Although the artist may have allowed such stories to go unchallenged early in his career, he vigorously protested them in public letters later on. In one such protest Paganini explained that the stories were a distortion of a dream had by his mother. In the dream, he said, the Savior (not the devil) came to his mother and told her that one prayer would be answered. She prayed that her son would become a great violinist, and her wish was granted.

16. Lockwood, "Robert Johnson" 26.

Bibliography

Interviews and Other Oral Sources

Edwards, David "Honeyboy." Onstage dialogue with Barry Lee Pearson during "workshop" program at 1991 the Festival of American Folklife, Smithsonian Institution, Washington, D.C.

Evans, David. Interview with Barry Lee Pearson, Clarksdale, Miss., 1993.

LaVere, Stephen C. Informal discussion with Bill McCulloch, Greenwood, Miss., April 2002.

Polk, Tommy. Informal discussion with Bill McCulloch, Hopson Plantation, Miss., May 2001.

Shines, Johnny. Onstage dialogue with Barry Lee Pearson during "workshop" program at the 1991 Festival of American Folklife, Smithsonian Institution, Washington, D.C.

———. Interview with Steve Abbott and Harry Tufts, Denver, Colo., April 1973.

Strachwitz, Chris. Telephone conversation with Barry Lee Pearson, 1999.

Sykes, Roosevelt. Interview with Barry Lee Pearson, Ann Arbor, Mich., August 1969.

Townsend, Henry. Onstage dialogue with Barry Lee Pearson during "workshop" program at the 1991 Festival of American Folklife, Smithsonian Institution, Washington, D.C.

Vernon, Paul. Telephone discussion with Barry Lee Pearson, April 2000.

Wardlow, Gayle Dean. Telephone interview with Bill McCulloch, February 2002.

Williams, Big Joe. Interview with Barry Lee Pearson, Ann Arbor, Mich., August 1969.

Nonprint Media

Can't You Hear the Wind Howl: The Life and Music of Robert Johnson. Documentary film produced and directed by Peter Meyer. Sweet Home Pictures, 1997.

Crossroads. Full-length motion picture directed by Walter Hill. Columbia Pictures, 1986.

Edwards, David "Honeyboy." *Crawling Kingsnake.* Sound recording Testament Records TCD 6002, 1997 (includes interview portions originally published by Pete Welding in *Blues Unlimited* and *Nothing but the Blues*). Testament Records TCD 6002, 1997.

————. *The World Don't Owe Me Nothing.* Sound recording. Earwig CD 4940, 1997.

Hellhounds on My Trail: The Afterlife of Robert Johnson. Documentary film directed by Robbert Mugge. Nonfiction Films and Mug-Shot Productions, 1999.

The Search for Robert Johnson. Documentary-style film produced for British commercial television and directed by Chris Hunt. Sony Music Video Enterprises, 1992.

Print Media

Alexie, Sherman. *Reservation Blues.* New York, N.Y.: Warner Books, 1995.

Banks, Russell. "The Devil and Robert Johnson: The Blues and the 1990s." *The New Republic* (Apr. 29, 1991): 27–31.

Barlow, William. *Looking Up at Down: The Emergency of Blues Culture.* Philadelphia, Pa.: Temple University Press, 1989.

Barnes, Bertram, and Glen Wheeler. "A Lonely Fork in the Road." *Living Blues* 94 (Nov.–Dec. 1990): 26–28.

Berendt, Joachim. *The Jazz Book: From New Orleans to Rock and Free Jazz.* 4th ed. New York, N.Y.: Lawrence Hill, 1975. Originally published as *Die Jazzbuch: von Rag bis Rock.* Frankfurt am Main: Fischer, Taschenbuch Verlag, 1953.

Blesh, Rudi. *Shining Trumpets: A History of Jazz.* New York, N.Y.: Knopf, 1946; repr., 1949; rev. ed., 1958.

Bockris, Victor. *Keith Richards: The Biography.* New York, N.Y.: Da Capo, 1998. Repr. of Poseidon ed. (1992).

Bragg, Rick, "Mississippi Man Ruled Sole Heir to Blues Legend." New York Times News Service release. *Chicago Tribune,* June 17, 2000, sect. A. (The story was published in many newspapers under different headlines.)

Brazier, Steve. "He Gone Straight to Hell. Knocked the Bottom Right Outta It." *Living Blues* 94 (Nov.–Dec. 1990): 10–11.

Calt, Stephen. "The Idioms of Robert Johnson." *78 Quarterly* 1, no. 4 (1989): 53–60.

————. "Robert Johnson Recapitulated." *Blues Unlimited* 86 (Nov. 1971): 12–14.

————. Liner notes. *The Roots of Robert Johnson.* Yazoo LP 1073.

Calt, Stephen, and Gayle Dean Wardlow. "Robert Johnson." *78 Quarterly* 1, no. 4 (1989): 40–50.

Caplin, Barbara. Liner notes. *Son House Delta Blues: The Original Library of Congress Sessions from Field Recordings, 1941–1942.* Biograph Records BCD118 ADD, 1991.

Charters, Samuel. *The Blues Makers.* New York, N.Y.: Da Capo, 1991.

———. *The Bluesmen.* New York, N.Y.: Oak, 1967.

———. *The Country Blues.* New York, N.Y.: Da Capo, 1959; rev. ed., 1975.

———. *The Poetry of the Blues.* New York, N.Y.: Oak, 1963.

———. *Robert Johnson.* New York, N.Y.: Oak, 1973.

Cheseborough, Steve, *Blues Traveling: The Holy Sites of Delta Blues.* Jackson: University Press of Mississippi 2001,

Cohn, Lawrence. "The Blues Did Not Die with Charlie Patton's Last Record!" *78 Quarterly* 1, no. 4 (1967; repr., 1992): 46–48.

———. "Son House, Delta Bluesman." *Saturday Review* 51, no. 39 (Sept. 28, 1968): 68–69.

Conway, Cecelia. *African Banjo Echoes in Appalachia.* Knoxville: University of Tennessee Press, 1995.

Cook, Bruce. *Listen to the Blues.* New York, N.Y.: Scribner's, 1973.

Corsello, Andrew. "John McEnroe." *Tennis* (Dec. 1999–Jan. 2000): 56.

Country Music Hall of Fame and Museum. *The Encyclopedia of Country Music: The Ultimate Guide to the Music.* New York, N.Y.: Oxford University Press, 1998.

Davis, Francis. "Blues Walking Like a Man: The Complicated Legacy of Robert Johnson." *Atlantic* 268 (Apr. 1991): 92–96.

———. *The History of the Blues.* New York, N.Y.: Hyperion, 1995.

Dixon, Robert M. W., John Godrich, and Howard Rye. *Blues and Gospel Records 1890–1943.* 4th ed. Oxford: Oxford University Press, 1997.

Donoghue, William E. *'Fessor Mojo's "Don't Start Me to Talkin."* Seattle, Wash.: Mojo Visions, 1997.

Driggs, Frank. Liner notes. *Robert Johnson: King of the Delta Blues Singers.* Columbia CL1654, 1961.

Edwards, David "Honeyboy," as told to Janis Martinson and Michael Robert Frank. *The World Don't Owe Me Nothing.* Chicago, Ill.: Chicago Review, 1997.

Ellison, Mary. *Extensions of the Blues Tradition.* New York, N.Y.: Riverrun, 1989.

Evans, David. Liner notes. *Black Boy Shine and Black Ivory King 1936–1937.* Document Records DOCD-5278, 1994.

———. "Ramblin David Evans: Robert Johnson—Pact with the Devil." Pts. 1–3. *Blues Review* 21 (Feb.–Mar, 1996): 12–13; 22 (Apr.–May 1996): 12–13 (retitled "Robert Johnson and the Supernatural"); 23 (June–July 1996): 12–13.

———. "Johnson, Robert Leroy." In *International Dictionary of Black Composers,* edited by Samuel A. Floyd Jr., 650–56. Chicago, Ill.: Fitzroy Dearborn, 1999.

———. *Tommy Johnson.* London: Studio Vista, 1971.

Ferris, Tim, "Robert Johnson: He Was Born, He Played Guitar, He Died." *Rolling Stone* (Feb. 4, 1971): 28.

Finn, Julio. *The Bluesman: The Musical Heritage of Black Men and Women in the Americas.* New York: Interlink Books, 1992.

Freeland, Tom. "'He Would Go Out and Stay Out': Some Witnesses to the Short Life of Robert Johnson." *Living Blues* 150 (Mar.–Apr. 2000): 42–49.

George, Nelson. *Hip Hop America.* New York, N.Y.: Penguin Books, 1998.

Goethe, Johann Wolfgang von. *Faust: A Tragedy.* New York, N.Y.: Norton, 2001.

Greenberg, Alan. *Love in Vain: The Life and Legend of Robert Johnson.* Garden City, N.Y.: Dolphin Doubleday, 1983.

Groom, Bob. *The Blues Revival.* London: Studio Vista, 1971.

———. "Robert Johnson: The Man behind the Music." *Blues World* 5 (Nov. 1965): 10–11.

———. "Standing at the Crossroads: Robert Johnson's Recordings." *Blues Unlimited* 118 (Mar.–Apr. 1976): 17–20; 119 (May–June): 11–14; 120 (Jul.–Aug.): 15–17; 121 (Sept.–Oct.): 20–21.

Guralnick, Peter. *Feel Like Going Home: Portraits in Blues and Rock 'n' Roll.* New York, N.Y.: Outerbridge, 1971.

———. "Johnny Shines—on the Road Again." *Blues World* 27 (Feb. 1976): 3–13.

———. "Robert Johnson and the Transformative Nature of Art." *Oxford American* 40:110–14.

———. "Robert Johnson in the '90s: A Dream Journey." In *1991 Festival of American Folklife Program Book,* 22–23. Washington, D.C.: Smithsonian Institution, 1991.

———. "Searching for Robert Johnson." *Living Blues* 53 (Summer–Autumn 1982): 27–41.

———. *Searching for Robert Johnson.* New York, N.Y.: Dutton, 1989.

Hammond, John. "Jim Crow Blues." Reprint of program notes to 1938 concert at which Johnson was supposed to appear. *New Masses* (Dec. 13, 1938): 27–28.

———. "Sight and Sound." *New Masses* 23 (June 8, 1937): 30.

———. Liner notes. *Spirituals to Swing: The Legendary Carnegie Hall Concerts of 1938/39.* Vanguard Jazz Showcase VRS 8523 and 8524, 1959.

Hammond, John, with Irving Townsend. *John Hammond on Record: An Autobiography.* New York, N.Y.: Ridge/Summit Books, 1977.

House, Son, as told to Julius Lester. "I Can Make My Own Songs." *Sing Out!* 15, no. 3 (July 1965): 38–45.

Hudgins, Tom. "Facts about the Robert Johnson Photographs." *78 Quarterly* 1, no. 4 (1989): 51.

Hyatt, Harry. *Hoodoo—Conjuration—Witchcraft—Rootwork.* Memoirs of the Alma Egan Hyatt Foundation. Hannibal, Mo.: Western, 1970.

Iglauer, Bruce, and staff. "Reconstructing Robert Johnson." *Living Blues* 2, no. 5 (Summer 1971): 6–9.

James, Steve. "Robert Johnson: The San Antonio Legacy." *Juke Blues* 12 (Spring 1988): 26–27.

Johnson, Henry (possibly a pseudonym for John Hammond). "Sight and Sound." *New Masses* 22 (Mar. 2, 1937): 27–29.

Klatzko, Bernard. "Finding Son House." *Blues Unlimited* 15 (Sept. 1964): 8–9.

Komara, Edward. "From the Archive" (Robert Johnson melodic precedent chart). *Living Blues* (Sept.–Oct. 1996): 12.

Kubik, Gerhard. *Africa and the Blues.* Jackson: University Press of Mississippi, 1999.

LaVere, Stephen. Liner notes. *Robert Johnson: The Complete Recordings.* Sony Columbia C2K 46222, 1990.

———. "Tying Up a Few Loose Ends." *Living Blues* 94 (Nov.–Dec. 1990): 31–33.

Law, Don. "Letter to Distributors." Submitted by Chris Strachwitz to *78 Quarterly* 10:7.

Leadbitter, Mike, ed. *Nothing but the Blues.* London: Hanover Books; New York, N.Y.: Oak, 1971.

Lee, Peter. "This Fella Y'all Looking For, Did He Die a Natural Death?" *Living Blues* 94 (Nov.–Dec. 1990): 2.

LeRoux, Charles. "American Odyssey: Seeking the Roots of Our Music." *Miami Herald,* July 2, 1978, Lively Arts sect.

Levet, Jean-Paul. "Stones in My Passway: Les Pratiques Magiques dans le Blues." *Soul Bag* 156 (Autumn 1999): 32–33.

Lipsitz, George. *The Possessive Investment in Whiteness: How White People Profit from Identity Politics.* Philadelphia, Pa.: Temple University Press, 1998.

Lockwood, Robert "Junior," compiled from an interview with Worth Long. "Robert Johnson, Blues Musician." In program book *1991 Festival of American Folklife,* 24–26. Washington, D.C.: Smithsonian Institution, 1991.

Lomax, Alan. *The Land Where the Blues Began.* New York, N.Y.: Pantheon Books, 1993.

———. Field notes, Lomax file. Library of Congress.

Marcus, Greil. *Mystery Train: Images of America in Rock 'n' Roll Music.* New York, N.Y.: Dutton, 1975.

———. "Walking in to a Room." *Village Voice* (Dec. 9, 1986): 63–66.

Miles, Milo. "Justice Hits the Charts at Last." *Boston Globe,* Dec. 7, 1990, Music sect.

N. A. "Forefathers: The Rock and Roll Hall of Fame." *Rolling Stone* 467 (Feb. 13, 1986): 48.

Napier, Simon, and Sonny Boy Williamson. "I Knew Robert Johnson." In *Nothing but the Blues,* edited by Mike Leadbitter, 96. London: Hanover Books, 1971.

Neff, Robert, and Anthony Connor. *Blues.* Boston, Mass.: David R. Godine, 1975.

Oakley, Giles. *The Devil's Music: A History of the Blues.* London: BBC, 1976.

Obrecht, Jas. "Robert Johnson." In *Blues Guitar: The Men Who Made the Music,* edited by Jas Obrecht, 2–13. San Francisco, Calif.: Miller Freeman, 1990.

O'Brien, Justin. "The Dark Road of Floyd Jones." *Living Blues* 58 (Winter 1983): 4–13; 59 (Spring 1984): 6–13.

———. "The Robert Johnson Photo." *Living Blues* 69 (1986): 9–10.

Oliver, Paul. *Blues Fell This Morning: The Meaning of the Blues.* New York, N.Y.: Horizon, 1960.

———. *Blues off the Record: Thirty Years of Blues Commentary.* New York, N.Y.: Da Capo, 1984.

———. *Conversations with the Blues.* New York, N.Y.: Horizon, 1965.

———. *The Story of the Blues.* New York, N.Y.: Chilton Books, 1969; repr., 1973.

O'Neal, Jim. "A Traveler's Guide to the Crossroads." *Living Blues* 94 (Nov.–Dec. 1990): 21–24.

———. "I Once Was Lost, but Now I'm Found: The Blues Revival of the 1960s." In *Nothing but the Blues,* edited by Lawrence Cohn, 347–87. New York: Abbeville, 1993.

O'Neal, Jim, Peter Lee, and others. "The Death of Robert Johnson." *Living Blues* 94 (Nov.–Dec. 1990): 8–20.

Palmer, Robert. *Deep Blues.* New York, N.Y.: Viking, 1981.

Pearson, Barry. "Ce Dell Davis' Story and the Arkansas Delta Blues." *Arkansas Review: A Journal of Delta Studies* 33, no. 1 (Apr. 2002): 3–14.

———. "Robert Johnson (1911–1938)." In *American Folklore: An Encyclopedia,* edited by Jan Harold Brunvand, 413–14. New York, N.Y.: Garland, 1996.

———. *"Sounds So Good to Me": The Bluesman's Story.* Philadelphia: University of Pennsylvania Press, 1984.

———. "Standing at the Crossroads between Vinyl and Compact Disks: Reissue Blues Recordings in the 1990s." *Journal of American Folklore* 105, no. 416 (Spring 1992): 215–26.

Perls, Nick. "Son House Interview—Part One." *78 Quarterly* 1 (1967): 59–61; repr., 1992.

Puckett, Newbell Niles. *The Magic and Folk Beliefs of the Southern Negro.* New York, N.Y.: Dover, 1969. Originally published as *The Folk Beliefs of the Southern Negro.* Chapel Hill: University of North Carolina Press, 1926.

Romanowski, Patricia, and Holly George-Warren, eds. *The New Rolling Stone Encyclopedia of Rock and Roll.* New York, N.Y.: Fireside, 1995.

Rooney, James. *Bossmen: Bill Monroe and Muddy Waters.* New York, N.Y.: Da Capo, 1971.

Ruskey, John. "Down in the Delta: Confusion at the Crossroads." *Blues Revue* 52 (Nov. 1999): 62–63.

Russell, Tony. *The Blues from Robert Johnson to Robert Cray.* New York, N.Y.: Schirmer Books, 1997.

Santelli, Robert. *The Big Book of Blues.* New York, N.Y.: Penguin Books, 1993.

Santoro, Gene. "Robert Johnson." *The Nation* (Oct. 8, 1990): 393–96.

Shea, Lisa. "The Complete Recordings of Robert Johnson." Picks and Pans . . . Song. *People Weekly* (Jan. 14. 1991).

Scherman, Tony. "The Hellhound's Trail: Following Robert Johnson." *Musician* 147 (Jan. 1991): 31–48.

———. "Phantom of the Blues." *American Visions* (June 1988): 21–24.

Shines, Johnny. "The Robert Johnson I Know." In *American Folk Music Occasional,* edited by Chris Strachwitz and Pete Welding, 30–33. New York, N.Y.: Oak, 1970.

Smith, Charles Edward, with Frederick Ramsey Jr., Charles Payne Rogers, and William Russell. *The Jazz Record Book.* New York: Smith and Durrell, 1942.

Szwed, John F. "Musical Adaptations among Afro-Americans." *Journal of American Folklore* 82, no. 324 (Apr.–June, 1969): 112–21.

Titon, Jeff Todd. "Living Blues Interview: Son House." *Living Blues* 31 (Mar.–Apr. 1977): 14–22.

Tooze, Sandra B. *Muddy Waters: The Mojo Man.* Toronto, Ont.: ECW, 1997.

Townsend, Henry, as told to Bill Greensmith. *A Blues Life.* Urbana: University of Illinois Press, 1999.

Wardlow, Gayle Dean. *Chasin' That Devil Music: Searching for the Blues.* Ed. Edward Komara. San Francisco, Calif.: Miller Freeman, 1998.

———. "Ledell Johnson Remembers His Brother Tommy." *78 Quarterly* 1 (1967): 63–65; repr., 1992.

———. "Robert Johnson: New Details on the Death of a Bluesman." *Guitar Player* (Nov. 1996): 29–32.

Waterman, Dick. "To Robert Johnson." *Living Blues* 94 (Nov–Dec. 1990): 42–43.

Waxman, John. Liner notes. *Robert Johnson: King of the Delta Blues Singers,* vol. 2. Columbia C30034, 1970.

Welding, Pete. "David 'Honey Boy' Edwards." *Blues Unlimited* 54 (June 1968): 3–13. Repr. in *Nothing but the Blues,* edited by Mike Leadbitter, 132–40. London: Hanover Books, 1971.

———. "Hell Hound on His Trail: Robert Johnson." *Blues Unlimited* 81 (Apr. 1971): 15; 82 (1971): 16–17; 83 (1971): 16–17. Repr. from *Down Beat's Music '66,* 73–76, 103. Chicago, Ill.: Maher, 1966.

———. "'I Sing for the People': An Interview with Bluesman Howling Wolf." *Down Beat* 34, no. 25 (Dec. 14, 1967): 20–21.

———. "An Interview with Muddy Waters." In *American Folk Music Occasional,* edited by Chris Strachwitz and Pete Welding 2–7. New York, N.Y.: Oak, 1970.

———. "Muddy Waters: Gone to Main Street." In *Bluesland: Portraits of Twelve*

Major American Blues Masters, edited by Pete Welding and Toby Byron, 130–57. New York, N.Y.: Penguin Books, 1991.

———. "Ramblin' Johnny Shines. *Living Blues* 22 (Jul.–Aug. 1975): 23–32; 23 (Sept.–Oct. 1975): 22–29.

———. "The Robert Johnson I Knew: An Interview with Henry Townsend." *Down Beat* 35, no. 22 (Oct. 31, 1968): 18, 32. Repr. as "Henry Townsend" in *Blues Unlimited* 64 (1969): 10–11; 65 (1969): 15; 66 (1969): 9.

———. Liner notes. *Robert Johnson: King of the Delta Blues Singers,* vol. 2. Columbia C30034, 1970 (these notes were not included with CBS reissue of the LP).

Wheeler, Brad. "Are the Blues Fixin' to Die?" *Toronto Globe and Mail,* July 7, 2001, R3.

Wilson, Alan. "Son House." *Blues Unlimited Collectors Classics* 14 (Oct. 1966).

Young, Al. "Robert Johnson: Toward a Robert Leroy Johnson Memorial Museum." In *Bluesland: Portraits of Twelve Major American Blues Masters,* edited by Pete Welding and Toby Byron, 69–97. New York, N.Y.: Dutton, 1991.

Index

A&R, 8, 11, 73, 78, 85, 116*n*9
Aberdeen, Mississippi, 113
Africa and the Blues, 63
Alexie, Sherman, 30, 62, 63, 88
American Record Corporation (ARC), 8, 117*n*1
Animals, the, 120*n*2
Arhoolie Records, 73, 124*n*26
Armstrong, Howard "Louie Bluie," 115*n*4
Arnold, Billy Boy, 120*n*2
Arnold, Kokomo, 74, 79
Asch, Moe, 21

Ballads, 72, 79, 126*n*10
Baptist Town, 9
Banks, Russell, 107
Barlow, William, 49, 100
Beatles, the, 33, 120*n*2
Bentonia, Mississippi, style, 84
Berendt, Joachim, 15, 118*n*14
"Black Gal, Why'n't You Comb Your Head," 72
"Black Mountain Blues," 66
Blesh, Rudi, 22–24, 25, 30, 31, 40, 55, 86, 110, 119*n*7, 126*n*9
"Blowin' in the Wind," 126*n*10
Blues: as autobiography, 29, 39, 85–86; idioms in, 66, 67–68, 81, 104–7, 124*n*22. *See also* Music, Johnson's
Blues Fell This Morning, 80, 124*n*22
Blues Guitar: The Men Who Made the Music, 53
Bluesmakers, The, 55
Bluesmen, The. See Finn, Julio
"Blue Spirit Blues," 66
Boyd, Eddie, 120*n*2
Bragg, Rick, 64
Broonzy, Big Bill, 23, 24

Brown, Ernest "Whiskey Red," 6
"Brown Skin Mojo Blues," 79
Brown, Willie, 7, 38, 48, 58, 60, 77, 88–89

Calt, Stephen, 2, 5, 49, 53, 68, 75, 82, 103, 115*n*7
Can't You Hear the Wind Howl? 53
"Captain George Did Your Money Come?" 72
"Casey Jones," 72
"Cat's Got the Measles," 124*n*21
Charters, Samuel, 2, 12, 15, 24–25, 29, 30, 31, 37–39, 40, 41, 42, 55, 67, 77, 88, 96, 108, 118*n*14, 120*n*10, 120*n*11, 122*n*13
Chasin That Devil Music, 87
Cheseborough, Steve, 123*n*8
Chess Records, 69
Clapton, Eric, 33, 40, 109
Clarksdale, Mississippi, 7, 61, 64, 112, 117*n*9
Coahoma County, Mississippi, 58, 60
Coffee, Willie, 98, 100–101, 105
Cohn, Larry, 54
Coleman, Estella, 8, 106
Columbia Records, 8, 27, 28, 33, 35, 46, 47, 54, 107, 108–9, 117*n*16
"Come on in My Kitchen," 43, 68, 74
Conversations with the Blues, 31, 46, 51
Conway, Cecilia, 95
Cooder, Ry, 43, 48, 87
Cook, Bruce, 33, 36–37
Country Blues, The, 24–25, 29, 37, 108
Craft, Calletta, 7
"Cross Road Blues," 28, 29, 35, 44, 57, 59, 74, 75–77, 79, 124*n*1
Crossroads (1986 movie), 43, 48, 62, 88, 94, 97, 99–100
Crossroads legend, 31, 37–38, 44–45, 48,

35, 36, 37, 39, 41, 44, 50, 65, 79, 80, 86,
124*n*1; lyrics discussed, 82–84; inter-
preted by Blesh, 22; interpreted by
Charters, 24–25, 37; interpreted by
Oliver, 32; relationship of, to style of
Skip James and others, 22, 82–84
"The Hellhound's Trail," 87
"Hell Is a Name for All Sinners," 66
Henderson, Sol, 15
Hip Hop America, 64
History of the Blues, The. See Davis,
Francis
Holiday, Harold (Black Boy Shine), 79
"Honeymoon Blues," 79
Hoodoo, 44, 67–69, 74, 79, 83, 85, 87,
121*n*28
Hooker, John Lee, 28, 120*n*2
Horton, Big Walter, 106
House, Son, 7, 14, 28, 31, 37–38, 45, 60, 61,
75, 87, 88–92, 93, 97, 99, 101, 103, 106,
108, 112, 120*n*11, 124*n*1, 125*n*15
Howling Wolf, 38
"Howling Wolf Blues No. 3," 83, 85
"Howling Wolf Blues No. 2," 84–85
Howling Wolf persona, 84
"Hungry Wolf Blues," 85
Hurt, Mississippi John, 108
Hyatt, Harry M., 95

"I Believe I'll Dust My Broom," 28, 44,
68, 74
"If I Had Possession over Judgment Day,"
28, 32, 75
"I'm a Steady Rollin' Man," 78, 84

Jackson, Mississippi, 8, 16, 82
Jackson, Papa Charlie, 124*n*21
James, Elmore, 26
James, Skip, 22, 75, 82, 84, 108
Jazz Book, The, 15
Jazz Record Book, The, 21
Jefferson, Blind Lemon, 23, 24, 61
Johnson, Claud, 64
Johnson, Henry. *See* Hammond, John
H., Jr.
Johnson, LeDell, 92–93, 99

Johnson, Lonnie, 66, 66, 79, 116–17*n*6
Johnson, Mary, 59–60, 122*n*13
Johnson, Noah, 6
Johnson, Robert L.: anecdotes about, 3,
12–13, 104–6; birth date(s), 6, 115*n*1;
and comparisons to literary figures,
36, 51; and defective eye, 6, 31, 119*n*6;
as folk artist, 2, 20–21, 24, 27–28, 78; as
inventor of rock and roll, 33–34, 36, 40,
55, 120*n*2; as mystery, 1, 2, 4, 28, 47, 54,
55; photos of, 46–48, 121*n*2; on postage
stamp, 48, 78; psychoanalyses of, 25, 31,
41–42; shyness, 2, 12–13. *See also*
Crossroads legend; Death and burial;
Music; Recordings; Shines, Johnny
Johnson, Tommy, 88, 92–93
Jones, Floyd, 26, 46
Jooks, 9, 115*n*4
Jordan, Charlie, 66

"Kindhearted Woman Blues," 21, 29, 68,
74, 104
King of the Delta Blues Singers (1961),
27–29
Kingston Trio, 126*n*10
Komara, Edward, 48, 87–88, 89–90, 97
Kubik, Gerhard, 50, 63

Land Where the Blues Began, The, 58–
61, 63
"Last Fair Deal Gone Down," 18, 19, 20,
21, 74
LaVere, Stephen, 2, 5, 10, 47, 53, 73, 98, 99,
100–101, 117*n*16, 118*n*18, 119*n*6, 121*n*2,
125*n*31
Law, Don, 8, 11, 20, 31, 73, 79, 85; as
source of inaccurate information
about Johnson, 12–14, 17, 28–29, 37
Law, Don, Jr., 13
Leadbelly (Huddie Ledbetter), 18, 19, 24
"Lead Pencil Blues," 82
Lee, Peter, 54
Legba, 45, 48, 50, 76, 121*n*27
Leonard, Michael, 97
Lester, Julius, 88, 89, 90, 118–19*n*11
Levet, Jean-Paul, 92

BARRY LEE PEARSON, a professor of English and American studies at the University of Maryland at College Park, is the author of *Sounds So Good to Me: The Bluesman's Story* (1984), *Virginia Piedmont Blues: The Lives and Art of Two Virginia Bluesmen* (1990), and more than a hundred articles. In the 1980s he toured Africa and South America for the U.S. State Department, performing with the Piedmont artists John Cephas and Phil Wiggins as the Bowling Green Blues Trio.

BILL MCCULLOCH, a career journalist with more than twenty-five years in the newspaper business and ten as a freelance writer, collaborated with Barry Lee Pearson on three dozen articles on American blues artists for the *American National Biography* (1999). Himself a musician, he moonlighted in the 1970s and 1980s as Windy City Slim.

Music in American Life

Only a Miner: Studies in Recorded Coal-Mining Songs   *Archie Green*
Great Day Coming: Folk Music and the American Left
    R. Serge Denisoff
John Philip Sousa: A Descriptive Catalog of His Works   *Paul E. Bierley*
The Hell-Bound Train: A Cowboy Songbook   *Glenn Ohrlin*
Oh, Didn't He Ramble: The Life Story of Lee Collins, as Told to Mary
    Collins   *Edited by Frank J. Gillis and John W. Miner*
American Labor Songs of the Nineteenth Century   *Philip S. Foner*
Stars of Country Music: Uncle Dave Macon to Johnny Rodriguez
    Edited by Bill C. Malone and Judith McCulloh
Git Along, Little Dogies: Songs and Songmakers of the American
    West   *John I. White*
A Texas-Mexican *Cancionero:* Folksongs of the Lower Border
    Américo Paredes
San Antonio Rose: The Life and Music of Bob Wills
    Charles R. Townsend
Early Downhome Blues: A Musical and Cultural Analysis
    Jeff Todd Titon
An Ives Celebration: Papers and Panels of the Charles Ives Centennial
    Festival-Conference   *Edited by H. Wiley Hitchcock and Vivian Perlis*
Sinful Tunes and Spirituals: Black Folk Music to the Civil War
    Dena J. Epstein
Joe Scott, the Woodsman-Songmaker   *Edward D. Ives*
Jimmie Rodgers: The Life and Times of America's Blue Yodeler
    Nolan Porterfield
Early American Music Engraving and Printing: A History of Music
    Publishing in America from 1787 to 1825, with Commentary on
    Earlier and Later Practices   *Richard J. Wolfe*
Sing a Sad Song: The Life of Hank Williams   *Roger M. Williams*
Long Steel Rail: The Railroad in American Folksong   *Norm Cohen*
Resources of American Music History: A Directory of Source Materials
    from Colonial Times to World War II   *D. W. Krummel, Jean Geil,
    Doris J. Dyen, and Deane L. Root*

Understanding Charles Seeger, Pioneer in American Musicology
  Edited by Bell Yung and Helen Rees
Mountains of Music: West Virginia Traditional Music from
  Goldenseal Edited by John Lilly
Alice Tully: An Intimate Portrait *Albert Fuller*
A Blues Life *Henry Townsend, as told to Bill Greensmith*
Long Steel Rail: The Railroad in American Folksong (2d ed.)
  Norm Cohen
The Golden Age of Gospel *Text by Horace Clarence Boyer;
  photography by Lloyd Yearwood*
Aaron Copland: The Life and Work of an Uncommon Man
  Howard Pollack
Louis Moreau Gottschalk *S. Frederick Starr*
Race, Rock, and Elvis *Michael T. Bertrand*
Theremin: Ether Music and Espionage *Albert Glinsky*
Poetry and Violence: The Ballad Tradition of Mexico's Costa Chica
  John H. McDowell
The Bill Monroe Reader *Edited by Tom Ewing*
Music in Lubavitcher Life *Ellen Koskoff*
Zarzuela: Spanish Operetta, American Stage *Janet L. Sturman*
Bluegrass Odyssey: A Documentary in Pictures and Words, 1966–86
  Carl Fleischhauer and Neil V. Rosenberg
That Old-Time Rock & Roll: A Chronicle of an Era, 1954–63
  Richard Aquila
Labor's Troubadour *Joe Glazer*
American Opera *Elise K. Kirk*
Don't Get above Your Raisin': Country Music and the Southern Working
  Class *Bill C. Malone*
John Alden Carpenter: A Chicago Composer *Howard Pollack*
Heartbeat of the People: Music and Dance of the Northern Pow-wow
  Tara Browner
My Lord, What a Morning: An Autobiography *Marian Anderson*
Marian Anderson: A Singer's Journey *Allan Keiler*
Charles Ives Remembered: An Oral History *Vivian Perlis*
Henry Cowell, Bohemian *Michael Hicks*

The University of Illinois Press
is a founding member of the
Association of American University Presses.

───────────────────────────────

Composed in 9/13 Cheltenham
with Dizzy display
by Celia Shapland
for the University of Illinois Press
Designed by Paula Newcomb
Manufactured by Thomson-Shore, Inc.

University of Illinois Press
1325 South Oak Street
Champaign, IL 61820–6903
www.press.uillinois.edu